ADMIT ONE!
Your Guide to College Application

By G. Gary Ripple, Ph.D.
Dean of Admission
The College of William and Mary

Address editorial correspondence to:

Octameron Associates
P.O. Box 3437
Alexandria, VA 22302

Address bookstore inquiries regarding purchases and returns to:

Longman Trade
5 S 250 Frontenac Road
Naperville, IL 60540
Outside Illinois: 1–800–245–BOOK
Inside Illinois: Collect 1–312–983–6400

Printed in the United States of America
ISBN 0–917760–97–2

Dedication

To Susan: My best friend, my wife, and the dean of my life.

Table of Contents

Acknowledgments

This work could not have been completed without the generous assistance of several important people. Wendy Pearson typed the manuscript while Susan Ripple and Marianne Janack offered valuable editorial advice.

Special assistance in preparing the chapters on the college essay was generously offered by Pam Fay of St. Catherine's School in Richmond, Virginia and Pedro Arango of University Liggett School in Grosse Point Woods, Michigan. Richard DiBianca, a student intern, also assisted in the project.

Colleagues in admission who made valuable observations on the ways and means to a good interview include: Richard Skelton, Bucknell; Sam Missimer, Lehigh; Judy Lyons, Susan Dromey and Gail Gardner, Ohio Wesleyan; Jan Hersey, Connecticut College; Kathlynn Ciompi, Vanderbilt; Bill Mason, Bowdoin; and Charles Deacon, Georgetown.

To each of these wonderful friends, I will be forever grateful.

Introduction

First the bad news. Reading **Admit One** is no guarantee you'll be accepted by all the colleges to which you apply. Nor is it a guarantee the admission process will be completely without its pitfalls.

Now the good news. Reading **Admit One** will decrease your pre-college jitters. It will make the application process go more smoothly. It will help you find the college that's best for you. And, it will show you how to present yourself to the admission committee in a way that will increase your chances for acceptance.

Admit One is divided into six major parts. First, it talks about what features you should consider when selecting a college; size, location, academic emphasis, and student body. Second, it describes the campus visit; why it's important, how to organize your trip, and what to look for at each school you visit. Third, the book answers your questions about the college interview; it tells you what personal qualities the interviewer is looking for and helps prepare you for a wide variety of questions. Fourth, **Admit One** summarizes the most important aspects of the college application; teacher recommendations, extracurricular activities, grade point averages, SAT/ACT scores, and the essay. Fifth, the book simplifies writing the college essay; it shows you how to choose a topic and reviews some basic grammar. Most importantly, it tells you what an admission committee is hoping to read and illustrates this with examples of both good and bad essays.

And last, **Admit One** contains a variety of appendices; some contain sample interview questions, others contain useful worksheets.

Good luck!

PART I

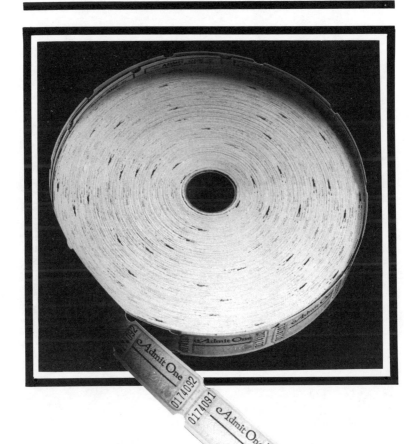

1

Selecting a College

 Whenever I complete a speaking assignment and ask for questions, I am always surprised when everyone wants to know how colleges select students. Very few people are interested in the more important question of how students select colleges even though students have more choices to make! After all, students have more than 3000 colleges and universities from which to choose, while schools usually have less than two applicants for each class opening.

THE IMPORTANCE OF COLLEGE SELECTION

Three decisions must be made before you can enroll at a college. First, you must decide to take the time and effort required to fill out the college's admission application. Second, the college must decide to admit you. Third, and MOST IMPORTANTLY, you must decide you want to enroll at the college. Careful readers will note that two of these three decisions are made by you the student and that the final and most important decision rests entirely in your hands.

Your college experience does not end at graduation. It will have some impact on what you do and who you are for the rest of your life. Your college experience will help you shape your values, select your friends, and establish your life goals. Even your career choice may be a direct result of decisions you once made on a college campus.

Clearly, where you go to college is one of the most important decisions you will ever make. It may also be one of your most difficult because frequently it is your first. Until now, all the major decisions of your life have probably been made by others, usually your parents. Now, you find yourself confronted with a decision of such magnitude that it will take you many months of thought to bring it to a full and complete resolution. During that time, you will receive lots of advice, most of it good, but it will be your responsibility to sift through the reams of papers and hours of conversation to make the final decision. Above all, it must be your decision because you are the one who must live with it. If someone else makes the decision for you, living with the outcome will be far more difficult.

CHOOSING A PLACE TO LIVE

Colleges love to survey their entering freshmen to find out why they chose their particular institution. Most entering freshmen list "academic reputation of the college" as the primary reason for their decision, even though the surveys show that the same students were considering other colleges of equal academic reputation. My guess is that the second reason, "good place to live," is probably the more important one. Choosing a college really does involve choosing a place to live—and not just choosing where you want to live but how and with whom.

There are several important characteristics to keep in mind when choosing your new "home":

Size. Are you looking for a relatively small self-contained institution? Do you want small classes taught by experienced professors? Do you relish the thought of rolling out of bed at three minutes before class and strolling next door into your classroom building without having to ride a bus to get there? Do you want a chance to play varsity basketball even though you're only 5'2"? Or would you prefer to be able to lose yourself in a large university? Do you like the feeling of

14

being a part of a large crowd at football games? Or concerts? Perhaps something in the middle; would a small university or a large college be an acceptable compromise?

Here is a list of information sources that will help you narrow your list of possible schools:

- **College Students.** Ask your friends who are home for their winter break to tell you about their schools. Keep in mind, they have probably just taken final exams, so their answers might be a bit slanted.
- **People Working in Your Field of Career Interest.** These people might be able to tell you what schools are strongest in your area of academic or professional interest.
- **High School Guidance Counselors.** Part of their job is to keep informed about colleges.
- **Your parents** (as well as your friends' parents). Most adults are a wealth of information. Be warned, however, if your parents went to college, they may just dust off an old yearbook and try to push their own alma mater.
- **College Fairs.** Those sponsored by the National Association of College Admission Counselors (NACAC) draw representatives from several hundred colleges. Admission is free, and you can pick up as much literature as you can carry.
- **High School College Information Nights.** Many high schools sponsor their own college fairs.
- **Commercial College Catalogues.** The most comprehensive is Orchard House's four volume *College Admissions Data Handbook* (check your guidance library). Another good one is Arco's *The Right College.*
- **Your Own Mailbox.** College admission offices will flood your mailbox with information if you so request when you take the SAT or ACT. Say ''yes,'' you want to be included in the College Board's Student Search Service or the American College Testing Program's Educational Opportunity Service.

Location. Here there are two subparts—the surrounding environment of the institution and its distance from your home. Urban institutions are much more diffused throughout a city and tend to have considerably more activities off-campus than on. A majority of the students are commuters (there may be more parking lots than dormitories) and you may have difficulty finding traditional campus life. In the rural institution, campus life is student life, and a great deal of emphasis is placed on extracurricular involvement. Students live in college housing and are selected primarily based on their potential to make contributions to the extracurricular life of the college. Once again, you may find "middle ground" in a suburban institution or one located in a large town where college life is supported by nearby cultural opportunities.

You must also make a conscious decision about how far away from home you want to travel. Part of the college experience is to break from the family and begin to define your unique individual identity. In most cases, the greater the distance, the easier it is to become truly independent and to establish that identity. I have, however, known students who attended institutions close to home who were able to accomplish the same feat by carefully negotiating such independence with their family prior to matriculation. Moms and dads agreed not to appear on campus in the middle of the week (or on Friday nights) while sons and daughters agreed not to show up at home five minutes before supper and expect a place to be set at the table.

Academic Emphasis. Do you want to attend a school dominated by undergraduates or an institution that focusses on research at the graduate level? Do you want a liberal arts-oriented institution, one with a technical or business orientation, or one that caters to all types of academic interests? An institution's personality and character are forged through its conception of its academic mission.

Extracurricular Activities. Almost as important as the school's academic emphasis is its offering of extracurricular activities. Do you want to attend a school with a crew team? A bridge club? A good drama club? A performing arts company? Are you a budding journalist or creative writer? Then look for an established school newspaper or literary review. What about social life? Does the campus have a film series? Fraternities? Sororities?

The Student Body. I believe a happy college living experience depends upon the composition of the student body. Every college's student body can be described in a way that will help you decide whether or not you would be happy living within such an environment. Do you want to attend a single sex or a coed institution? Is religious affiliation important? Who will be your friends? And where will they be from? What will be their academic backgrounds and how will their test profiles compare with yours? Do you want to be a big fish in a little sea, or a little fish in a big sea? In other words, do you want to be among the brightest and best prepared, among the least prepared, or would you like to fall somewhere in the middle?

Financial Concerns. Even in these days of rapidly increasing tuitions, I feel that the cost of an institution should be one of your least important considerations as you define your ideal institution. The amount a college must charge for tuition and fees is largely unrelated to the other characteristics which are important to you. Private colleges have varying endowments and public institutions receive large subsidies from state governments. By and large, these matters bear little on the quality of education. I have found that the most expensive colleges also have the most generous financial aid budgets and the willingness to consider individual family circumstances while the least expensive may not offer the living conditions which make it possible for you to be a happy and successful student. By all means, find the ideal college first and worry about financial aid second. Also remember, your family's contribution to college costs, as determined by the Congressional Method, is not dependent upon the cost of an institution. It is the same, no matter what school you plan to attend.

All of these characteristics can and should be taken into account as you narrow your choice from among the more than 3,000 possibilities. In a way, choosing a college is like walking into a clothing store and looking for a new sports jacket or dress. If you are confronted with 3,000 possibilities, it helps to have some idea of what you are looking for—color, style, size—before you enter the store. Otherwise, you will be hopelessly confused by the plethora of possibilities. Once you have defined your need, you are ready to shop. Similarly, once you have determined the general characteristics of your ideal college, you are ready to begin the process of visiting college campuses and meeting with admission officers for the purpose of selecting a college that is right for you.

Here is a list of information sources that will help you narrow your list of possible schools:

- **College Students.** Ask your friends who are home for their winter break to tell you about their schools. Keep in mind, they have probably just taken final exams, so their answers might be a bit slanted.
- **People Working in Your Field of Career Interest.** These people might be able to tell you what schools are strongest in your area of academic or professional interest.
- **High School Guidance Counselors.** Part of their job is to keep informed about colleges.
- **Your parents** (as well as your friends' parents). Most adults are a wealth of information. Be warned, however, if your parents went to college, they may just dust off an old yearbook and try to push their own alma mater.
- **College Fairs.** Those sponsored by the National Association of College Admission Counselors (NACAC) draw representatives from several hundred colleges. Admission is free, and you can pick up as much literature as you can carry.
- **High School College Information Nights.** Many high schools sponsor their own college fairs.
- **Commercial College Catalogues.** The most comprehensive is Orchard House's four volume *College Admissions Data Handbook* (check your guidance library). Another good one is Arco's *The Right College.*
- **Your Own Mailbox.** College admission offices will flood your mailbox with information if you so request when you take the SAT or ACT. Say ''yes,'' you want to be included in the College Board's Student Search Service or the American College Testing Program's Educational Opportunity Service.

PART II

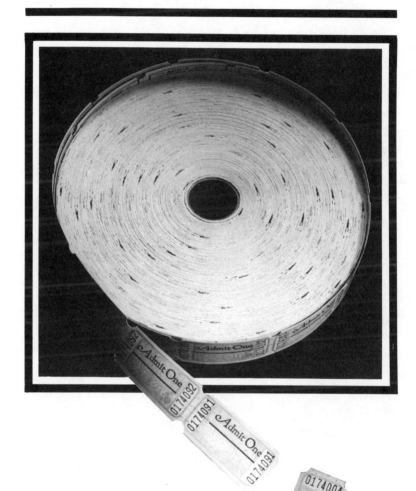

2

Visiting a College

Buying shoes has always been a problem for me. I am one of those poor souls (sorry) with an unusual size, one that shoe stores rarely stock in great supply or with any diversity of style. A few years ago I tired of trudging around looking for shoes in shoe stores and succumbed to the temptation of ordering a pair of shoes through a mail-order catalogue. When my shoes arrived, they were the wrong color (at least they didn't look at all like their picture), they were of inferior quality and, worst of all, they did not fit. To this day, I am constantly reminded by my dear wife, Susan, that "you can't buy shoes through the mail." And so it is with colleges. There is just no way to shop for a four-year $25,000–$75,000 college education by looking at catalogues and viewbooks produced by the institutions themselves. After a while, the copy all sounds the same and the photographs all look identical (obviously taken by the same creative photographer; a person who earns his or her living by making any campus look like the Taj Mahal). You can turn this into kind of a game. As you you read through college handbooks, count how many schools boast having the oldest or first of something (for example, the oldest microscope in continuous use or the first recognized program in dandelion breeding). Also count how many times you see autumn leaves or snow capped mountains (a bright blue sky is mandatory, unless it is early morning or late evening in which case expect to see a colorful sunrise or sunset). Finally, observe student activity. How many people are playing frisbee or lolling about on the campus green between classes?

Commercial college handbooks are no better as they, too, are based on information provided by colleges and universities. Large publishing enterprises such as Barron's and Peterson's also suffer from an additional malady: Their material is frequently out of date by the time it appears on bookstore shelves.

The so-called "insiders' guides" are fun to read but are no more reliable. They suffer from the questionable nature of their sources... usually students at the colleges who base much of their impressions on rumors and have the natural tendency to inflate the information beyond any useful dimension.

With all the problems inherent in written accounts of what colleges are actually like, it becomes extremely important for the potential student to get out on the road and visit colleges that sound like they just might be a good fit. After all, seeing is believing.

A campus visit enables you to stroll the grounds, inspect the interiors of buildings, read the student newspaper to learn of important campus issues, check bulletin boards for campus activities, visit the student union or local coffee shop, try the dining hall food and meet the people with whom you might some day be living (remembering, however, that you cannot meet everyone at the school, and those with whom you do converse are usually expressing personal opinions). By experiencing the many vibrations which emanate from a college campus, you can make some relatively well-informed decisions about the quality of life within the walls of that particular institution.

Campus visits also allow you to take a formally organized campus tour and meet a member of the college admission program who can answer your questions and interpret admission policies. Much more will be said about the interview later in this publication.

The purpose of the campus visit is to give you a chance to try on a school—to see if it fits. As you stroll the grounds, you should ask yourself "can I see myself here?" Is this a place I can be happy living for a few years? If your final choice comes down to splitting hairs, it is the intuitive feelings you gain from a campus visit that can and should enable you to resolve your dilemma. If you have followed the important steps, gathering all the facts and weighing the pros and cons, you can rely on your inner feelings in the final analysis of your alternatives.

PARENTS IN THE PROCESS

In some families, sons and daughters simply assume mom and dad will accompany them as they visit colleges. In other families, this assumption is not made and can generate great debate and many hard feelings. In my opinion, if parents are going to be asked to contribute to the cost of your education, they should certainly be invited to participate in the campus visits. In fact, I usually advocate a team approach (moms, dads, even brothers and sisters) believing that the more pairs of eyes and ears a team has, the more information that can be gleaned from the visit. Even if your parents are not going to contribute to the cost of your education, they should be included in the visit, as they are likely to be called upon to provide other types of support, namely emotional support whenever things are not going as well as you would like. It must always be understood, however, that the student will be making the decision with regard to what is best for him or her.

This is not to say that having parents along is always a positive experience. Students should make certain they have some time alone with both college students and the interviewer during their campus visit. The reason for this should be obvious: Answers to questions may vary depending on the composition of the audience. For example, a college student may not be completely honest with you if your parents are listening in on the conversation. Even worse, you may not be completely honest in your answers when speaking with a member of the admission staff. For this reason, I suggest parents be given some special assignments independent of the student during the time spent on

23

campus (for example, "checking out" the library or the bookstore). That way, parents can enhance their overall contribution to the data-gathering process while giving the student the opportunity to talk about matters which may be of a more personal nature.

You, however, know your parents best. If they are likely to take control of the interview, or if they make you tense, you might be better off visiting schools on your own. I do not suggest visiting colleges with friends unless you can agree on an itinerary that benefits all of you. Remember, the primary purpose of the campus visit is to gather information!

PLANNING THE VISIT

You must consider several factors in planning the visit. What is the best time of year to make the trip? How far ahead should you establish the itinerary? Should you have the interview before or after the admission decision has been made? Are weekdays better than weekends? How many colleges should you visit in one day? In one week?

Once you have formulated the list of colleges you want to visit, you should get on the telephone and talk directly with the admission office appointment secretaries at least three weeks in advance of your intended visit (The amount of advance time required will vary depending on the time of year). As you begin to work out an itinerary, plan to spend one day and one night at each school on your list. Also, try not to visit your first choice school first. I recommend you "practice" on a safety school.

It is important that YOU decide which schools to visit and make the plans to coordinate those visits. Do not allow others to assume a lion's share of all of the fun that comes with calling the institutions and making the appropriate arrangements. I am always impressed by students who call themselves, rather than sitting back until their exasperated parents finally step in and try to make the arrangements for them.

Be sure to use the telephone instead of writing a letter when you contact the colleges. Some even have a toll-free 800 number that will save you money and put you in direct contact with the person who makes the appointments. To see if the school has a toll-free number, call information at 1-800-555-1212.

In considering what time of year to visit colleges, one must take into account the trade-offs involved. For example, interviews are easier to schedule in the early summer when the admission staff is usually less harried and in a better frame of mind for conducting a relaxed informal conversational interview. But remember, early summer is often the time when colleges are devoid of students and it will be difficult for you to evaluate them in terms of what life is like during the hectic fall and spring semesters. When I was taking my own two sons on their college tour, I elected to visit colleges in the summer because it was relatively easy to plan an itinerary that included ten institutions in just five days. Such a tour through three states would be extremely difficult to schedule in October or November because that is when most people want to visit. Ironically, it is also when the admission staff is less accessible because they are on the road visiting you in your high school and at college fairs. Thus, I believe it best to make preliminary visits to colleges in the summer and plan a follow-up visit to your first choice institutions later on in the process. A follow-up visit without the formal interview allows you be be more casual in dress and better able to move with the flow of student life as a visitor to classes and social gatherings.

Unfortunately, this ideal schedule does not often work. Even if it were not expensive and time consuming, the onslaught of college information you will receive during the fall of your senior year is likely to change your thoughts and goals so much that an itinerary carefully planned in April will be of little use to you in October.

The only really bad time to visit colleges is during their exam periods. Social life is at a minimum, classes do not meet, and students and faculty will have little time for your questions.

Most colleges would like you to visit during the week rather than on weekends. This is because we who work in admission offices are human and like to spend weekends and holidays with our friends and families. Realizing this may create hardships for others, most colleges are open on Saturday mornings and will provide group presentations and tours to those who find it more convenient to visit then. You will best be served, however, if you can make it on a weekday. Besides, on weekdays you are better able to observe the academic life of the school (as opposed to the social life), and isn't that your primary interest?

Earlier I mentioned the importance of calling the college rather than writing a letter to request information and an appointment. By speaking directly with the appointment secretary, you will be able to accomplish the following:

1. Learn if the day and time you would like to visit are convenient. If you have scheduled an interview, ask for a written confirmation of your appointment.

2. Find out if a separate reservation is needed for a campus tour. If it is, be sure you know when the tour begins and if your name is included on the list.

3. Ask to have information about the college mailed to you in advance of the trip. You will use this (along with any other information you have put together) to make a list of important points you wish to convey about yourself and questions you would like to ask the people you meet at the institution.

4. Ask if you need to bring anything with you. Some interviewers would like you to bring a resume or unofficial copy of your high school transcript and test scores.

5. Find out what special accommodations might be available, such as dining hall meal tickets and overnight dormitory facilities. If the school does not provide dorm space, ask about other overnight accommodations (appointment secretaries might be willing to make reservations on your behalf).

6. Find out about upcoming campus events. Students interested in theater might want to schedule their visit at a time they can see a school play. Similarly, future coxwains might want to schedule their visit around a crew regatta.

7. Ask about driving distances and times between your home, the college, and other institutions that may be on your tour. You might also ask what other colleges are located nearby or what attractions

may be worth seeing while you are in the area. Many visitors to The College of William and Mary, for example, combine their trip with a tour of Colonial Williamsburg, a day splashing at the beach, or the excitement of nearby Busch Gardens. Sometimes, other attractions give younger members of the family something to do while you are engaged in the more important business of scrutinizing the college and its offerings.

As you can see, a successful campus visit and interview requires a great deal of advance planning. Your itinerary must allow you enough time to visit each college and you must make certain that a personal appointment will be available to you when you are at each college. Note: As a courtesy, tell your high school teachers about your plans, and ask them about making up missed schoolwork.

Although you must leave room in your planning for spontaneity and just plain being yourself, it is wise to prepare a brief plan of goals and objectives for each institutional visit. This plan has two major parts: First, what do you wish to learn about the institution while you are there and, second, what would you like to have the institution know about you as a result of your visit? The first area is essential to your understanding of the institution and what it can offer you. The second is the beginning of the important process by which colleges assess your character traits. These impressions will later become a part of your college application. In the weeks and months ahead, you and the colleges will be making important decisions about each other. For those decisions to be accurate and well-considered, it is essential you get to know as much about one another as possible. Only in that way will good decisions be made by each party.

WHAT DOES A GOOD COLLEGE VISIT INCLUDE?

Your first stop in any visit should be the admission office. There, you can introduce yourself if you are scheduled for an interview or tour, or you can pick up a campus map if you plan to explore on your own.

Most importantly, a productive visit depends upon your being able to schedule enough time to absorb something of each campus, especially if you are traveling a great distance and going to much time and expense in making the call. The ingredients of a successful visit include the following:

A personal interview. This will be discussed in great detail in the next two chapters.

A campus tour. In addition to learning a lot of college fun facts, you should see a mixture of campus buildings—classrooms, laboratories, computer facilities, athletic facilities, dormitories, the library, health clinic, dining hall, student center, music hall, theater, and art gallery. Be sure to see the insides of some buildings, especially if you only have a short time to spend on campus.

A visit to at least one class in an academic area of interest. While you are in the classroom, observe the students. Are they attentive? Bored? Are they participating in class discussion? Remember, all colleges have good and bad teachers. To make certain your first college lecture is interesting, read through course evaluations or ask students to tell you their favorites. Course evaluations are generally written by students at the end of each semester. Ask someone in the admission office where you might find them.

A conversation with a professor in your area of interest. Again, read course evaluations or talk to students to find a chatty professor. Some are better with students than others. Make certain you visit during scheduled office hours so you don't disrupt his or her work.

At least one meal in the campus dining hall. This is absolutely critical as no one can go four years without food. Investigate your options. Does the dining hall have a salad bar? Soup? Ice cream? Peanut butter and jelly? (These are all fairly safe, so on days when the menu reads "Chef's surprise" you needn't go hungry). Does it serve a vegetarian meal? Kosher food? What about alternative food spots? Is there a late night grill for the midnight munchies?

An overnight stay in a dormitory. This is the best way to get to know students and the social life of a school. What do people do for fun? Do they go to football games, listen to chamber music, or both? Are fraternities and sororities the center of campus life? Or is it the library? If possible, ask to stay with a sophomore or junior. They are likely to know more about the school than a freshman (especially if you are visiting in the fall).

A thorough study of college information. Make certain to pick up at least one application form.

Reading a recent copy of the student paper and weekly calendar. This will give you an idea of campus issues (divesting in South Africa, crowded dormitories...) and activities.

Reading an alumni magazine. This will supplement information from the college's placement office to give you an idea of what happens to the school's graduates. Do they all become tax attorneys and investment bankers, or do some trek through Nepal and write prize winning poetry? As you read the magazine, remember the alumni who are mentioned may not be entirely representative. For the most part, they are limited to those who take the time to send in their accomplishments.

Visiting the library. Does it seem like a comfortable place to study? Can you reserve a study carrel? Are there rooms for group meetings? How many copy machines do you see? Do they work? What are the library hours? Is there someplace you can study 24-hours a day? Does the library stay open during vacations so students can finish overdue term papers? Are there comfortable reading chairs? Does the library have a subscription to your hometown newspaper (this can help alleviate any homesickness experienced during the first part of your freshman year)? Does the school have separate departmental libraries?

Time in the surrounding community. Read the local newspaper to learn more about the school's environment. Is the town within walking distance? Does it have movie theaters? Can you get pizza or Chinese food delivered? Do you see any used book, clothing, or record stores? What about banks and grocery stores?

Plenty of free time to stroll the campus and observe all ongoing activities. As you wander about the campus, observe the students, the way they dress, their interaction with classmates. Make a point of stopping in any buildings not visited on the campus tour. What kinds of books and magazines are carried in the school's bookstore? The New York Review of Books or the National Enquirer? Does the school have a women's center? An art museum?

Not all these ingredients are available or possible all the time. For example, classes are not usually held on Saturdays and some institutions frown on strangers spending the night in the dormitories. Many colleges, however, will offer incentives (for example, free meal tickets and an overnight host program) to make certain that prospective applicants do visit and make the most of their opportunity. Again, your telephone call to the appointment secretary should include the question "what special opportunities do you offer to visiting prospective applicants?"

FOLLOWING UP THE CAMPUS VISIT

I recommend all students do two things upon completing a campus visit. First, write down your impressions of the institution. Second, write a thank you letter to your interviewer or tour guide.

If you visit a lot of colleges (more than five) you will discover that their many "unique" features gradually melt together in your memory. This is why I recommend you keep a diary of all of your visits. Immediately after you leave a campus, you should scribble down all of your impressions from the visit. What features did you like? What areas did you see as weaknesses? Establish a rating scale and use it to rank those colleges which you have visited. Continually revise their order as you gather more information and visit other campuses.

No doubt, additional questions about each college will come to mind after you leave. It is a good idea to write these down and send them to your college interviewer as part of a general thank you note which expresses your appreciation for the time spent and the advice you received from the interview itself. Thank you letters should be typed on plain paper, or neatly handwritten on tasteful stationary (no scented roses, please). Your interviewer will remember those who follow-up with a note and will take whatever time is necessary to answer the additional questions you have posed in your follow-up letter.

Some families bring a camera and take pictures to help make each campus memorable many weeks after the visit. You should pose in some of the pictures so when the time comes for you to decide where you ultimately want to see yourself, you will remember just how you looked on each campus.

If possible, you should make a follow-up trip to the one or two colleges at the top of your list, especially if you are successful in gaining admission. Colleges change from season to season as will your own thoughts and concerns.

IF YOU CANNOT VISIT COLLEGES

If you are not able to visit the colleges that interest you, ask your counselor to help you find a VCR and a video of the school. Nearly a dozen organizations now make such videos available, both to schools and individuals. As you watch, remember these films have been prepared by public relations professionals, and should be viewed with the same skepticism usually reserved for "use our perfume, and men will bring you flowers" advertising.

You should also attend college fairs and high school college information nights, arrange for an interview with an alumni in your area, and finally, speak with admission representatives when they visit your high school.

It's All Academic

1. At what university might you be presented with a rodeo scholarship?
2. At what southern school might you be presented with a bagpipe scholarship?
3. What school founded both Phi Beta Kappa and the Honor System of conduct?
4. What library at what school placed the one millionth Interlibrary Loan request?
5. At what school did scholars first split the atom, discover the speed of light, and develop the field of sociology?
6. What prestigious midwestern university was founded with no faculty, no campus, no students, no buildings, and only $9.92 in its treasury?
7. In what year was the first College Board exam held?

PART III

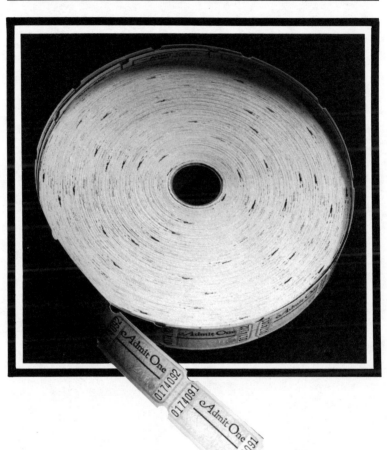

3

The College Interview

 People obviously realize the importance of the interview in the college selection process as they go to great pains—both in time and expense—to make certain they receive a personal audience at the colleges in which they have the greatest interest. Beyond this, however, few people are adequately prepared for the interview itself. In the many years I have served as an admission officer, I have conducted several thousand personal interviews. Each year, I am always astounded by the number of candidates (nearly eighty percent) who waste the opportunities an interview can provide. This is particularly alarming when you think of all the arrangements required to make interviews possible.

HOW IMPORTANT IS AN INTERVIEW?

An interview is important for several reasons.

First, when you make the time and effort to be present for the interview, you demonstrate a sincere interest in the institution. You are saying "I respect you and value your institution's education. I want to learn more about you and hope you want to learn more about me."

Second, the interview gives you an opportunity to learn firsthand about the school's academic philosophy and admission policy. You can glean important facts, and confirm or dispel possible rumors. You can gain a better understanding of how the selection process works which, in turn, will enable you to make yourself a better candidate.

Third, the interview allows you to present yourself in a very personal way. This can be good or bad. If you are articulate and outgoing with a depth of personal insight that makes you an attractive candidate, you should make certain to interview at every college in which you have a strong interest. If, however, you come across as arrogant, or shy, or truly ill at ease in the presence of authority figures, you may wish to forego the interview experience because of its possibly damaging effects on your candidacy.

Most colleges will tell you the interview is not an important part of the selection process, that it's only real use is to confirm the recommendations of teachers and counselors, and that it is an imperfect method of evaluating a student. This is not to say they care any less about the student as an individual. Rather, these schools feel students should take the time they otherwise would have devoted to the interview process and use it to extend their campus visits. The admission staff would use the time they save to run additional informational sessions.

All this aside, a recent study conducted by the College Board, Educational Testing Service, and nine selective private institutions concluded that interviews can be very important, especially for those who fall in the broad middle range of candidates who are qualified but not exceptional (Personal Qualities and College Admission, College Entrance Examination Board, 1982). At the same time, your interview may provide important information which will help you in the final decision regarding your choice of college. Therefore, plan to have personal interviews and take the steps necessary to make your interviews highly productive and extremely worthwhile. Don't be like most of the people I interview who waste the opportunity to make their interview a critical factor in the decisions made by them and the colleges of their choice.

WHAT ARE THEY LOOKING FOR?

The admission staff wants to gather information on the "total" student; academic and educational potential, motivation, and personality traits. More specifically, the skilled interviewer will be collecting evidence of the following:

Intellectual Promise. This is a favorite area of faculty interviewers who see in each prospective student a potential colleague, one who will join with them in the pursuit of knowledge. Questions about favorite books or favorite courses are often attempts to measure your level of intellectual curiosity or determine your interest in learning as an end in itself.

Motivation. Your interviewer will try to measure your inner drive and will probably do so by asking you to list some of your important accomplishments. When doing so, you should explain why each accomplishment was important.

Energy Level. Are you laid back or high strung? Do you bounce out of bed in the morning or do you need a blast of caffeine? Are you out dancing until midnight or do you run out of steam before sunset?

Stability. Your ability to control your emotions and demonstrate consistent unflappability are on display throughout the interview. In other words, don't curl your lip when asked a particularly difficult question.

Sense of Humor. Be ready to crack a smile if your interviewer is in a good mood or detects that you might be too tense and tries to loosen you up a little bit. Don't be afraid to laugh (that is, if the interviewer has said something amusing).

Values. No "right" or "wrong" is being tested. Your interviewer simply wants to know what values you will bring with you to the campus. This should not be misconstrued as an attempt to purge the student body of undesirable elements. Be relaxed and prepared to state your beliefs with firmness and conviction.

Interest in the Institution. This is hard to fake. You are here either because it was your idea or because it was someone else's. There is nothing wrong with admitting you are here on a fact-finding mission and have yet to develop any strong desire to attend the college. Be leery, however, of being candid to the point of saying you are only there because someone sent you.

Articulation. Your ability to speak well using good diction can make a very positive impression on the interviewer. Role playing with a friend is terrific practice, but beware of letting your answers sound overrehearsed. Pure spontaneity can be a big plus if you are clear in what you have to say and concise in how you say it.

Integrity. This should be self-explanatory but there are many ways of being dishonest in an interview. Little white lies (for example, "my counselor told me not to tell anyone what my SAT scores are") can be just as damaging to the interviewer's overall opinion as outright falsehoods.

Independence. How well would you cope in an unusual or foreign situation without family and close friends? Evidence of your independence can usually be brought out with questions such as "how do you spend your free time" and "have you ever been away from home for a relatively long period of time?"

Leadership. Every college hopes to enroll a certain number of students who will generate activity and provide the student leadership so necessary for successful extracurricular activities. The types of positions you have held (elected or appointed) and how well you have carried out your responsibilities will be an important topic in most college interviews.

Personality. As with values, there are no rights or wrongs in this area. Your interviewer wants to measure your basic approach to everyday life in an attempt to determine if you are a good fit with the personalities of the current student body. Not being so does not necessarily mean a denial of admission. Being different may actually be a plus, but you never know until the final analysis.

Originality. This is particularly important now as so many young people appear to be governed by peer pressures to conform. Here is where a great deal of prior thinking can make your interview a very productive experience. Take some time to think about those aspects of your character which make you unique. Any expressions of your creativity should be brought into the conversation so they have an opportunity to be recognized by the institution.

Self-Image. Your body language is often a tip-off about how you really feel about yourself. Many admission officers feel there is no more important character trait to succeeding in college than a healthy self-image. This is what brings you through the difficult days every student has during the college years.

Confidence. Once again, your body language is a good sign of your attitude toward new and challenging tasks. Be careful not to sound boastful, egotistical, or overconfident. At the same time, do express your positive attitude toward new and challenging opportunities.

Preparation. Your interviewer will expect some familiarity with the college and its admission process and will attempt to discover how much you learned about the institution prior to your visit. Being well prepared (taking time to learn about the institution) will demonstrate your sincerity and enable the interviewer to go into higher levels of discussion much more quickly. Poorly prepared students (those who ask whether the school requires SAT scores) usually lose a lot of points in the interview process.

Other areas that might be of interest to the institutional representative include your organizational skills, sincerity, commitment to task and social conscience. These will vary with the institution and may or may not become critical to decisions that will be made later on in the selection process.

HOW TO PREPARE FOR AN INTERVIEW

A successful interview depends on your knowledge of yourself and of the college. To prepare you to talk about yourself, I recommend forming a list of adjectives that describe your personality (conscientious, reserved, lively, assertive), your strengths (intelligent, creative, articulate, athletic), and your weaknesses (sloppy, timid, obstinate—nothing too negative). Also, give some thought to your goals and your values; what is truly important to you? Now you're ready to answer questions, both of an academic and a personal nature. To prepare you to talk about the college, I recommend reading the college catalogue from cover to cover. After doing so you should know something about the diversity of the school's faculty and curriculum, the difficulty of its admission and graduation requirements, and the variety of its student services, living facilities, and special programs (year abroad, writer-in residence). Now you're ready to ask the questions. For instance, if the health service hours are limited to Monday through Friday from 9 to 5, find out what happens if you get sick on weekends. If the entire economics department received their doctorates from MIT in approximately the same year, ask whether the department teaches both liberal and conservative theory.

WHAT REALLY HAPPENS IN AN INTERVIEW?

The length of time set aside for personal interviews varies from school to school (usually thirty to forty-five minutes), and does not reflect the attitude of the school toward you the student. In other words, if the admission dean from Taciturn Tech spends 35 minutes with you, and the dean from Chatty U. spends 45, you should not assume the Chatty dean liked you better.

The actual format of the college interview also varies from school to school (or even within the same school) due to individual differences of personality and objectives. There is, however, a general consensus among college admission officers as to what an interview should accomplish and how it should be conducted. An interview nearly always has four parts. First, it includes time for breaking the ice. Then, the interviewer will launch into general conversation; questions about your high school experience and your interest in the college. Third, you will get to ask your questions. And last, after completion of the private one-on-one phase, the interviewer will ask for questions from mom or dad.

INTRODUCTORY PROTOCOL

Typically, you and your parents will be seated in the lobby of the admission office waiting for your interviewer to come out and introduce him or herself. When you hear your name called, stand and greet the

40

interviewer with a firm handshake and a friendly relaxed look on your face. A firm handshake is best for both boys and girls. Be prepared to introduce the interviewer to anyone who has accompanied you on the visit. If either or both of your parents has a different last name, say so with clarity and firmness (this will save the embarrassment of addressing your parents by the wrong name). The interviewer will chat for a moment with your parents before excusing the two of you to go into an interview office for the private one-on-one phase of the process. It is important for you to speak with your interviewer alone and not let your parents do your talking for you.

BEGINNING THE INTERVIEW AND A WORD ABOUT BODY LANGUAGE

Upon entering the interview room, take whatever chair is offered. DO NOT ATTEMPT TO MOVE THE CHAIR ANY CLOSER TO THE INTERVIEWER. In all probability the chair has been strategically placed a distance at which the interviewer is comfortable talking with you. Just as "actions speak louder than words," the nonverbal behavior you exhibit will be the yardstick by which the interviewer measures your words, attitude, and intentions. Be aware of your sitting posture. Is it tense or relaxed, closed or open? Assume a natural sitting position, one that is comfortable but appropriate to the situation. Sitting rigidly on the edge of your chair indicates uneasiness or over-anxiousness. Slouching conveys disinterest. And sitting with arms and legs tightly crossed suggests hostility or overaggression. Holding your body alert, hands resting easily on the chair or in your lap and legs crossed comfortably at the knees or ankles all suggest a receptive "open" attitude toward the interviewer and the interview process.

An interviewer's worst nightmare is trying to sustain a conversation with someone who responds monosyllabically or who stares disinterestedly out the window or rigidly at the floor. Eye contact implies forthrightness and is perhaps the single most expressive nonverbal message you will send. This does not mean you need to stare unflinchingly, but take care to meet the interviewer "eye to eye" both as he or she speaks to you and as you respond to questions.

41

The interview is your opportunity to add depth to your written application, to define aspects of your personality that may not be communicated through the written word. There is some truth in the cliche "it's not what you say but how you say it." The tone of your voice, its volume, and the inflection you use can either hold or lose the listener's attention. Avoid mumbling, speaking in monotone and giving one-syllable responses. You deserve to be heard. Attentive body posture, appropriate eye contact and the overall quality of verbal expression will help to ensure that you hold your audience.

GETTING THE INTERVIEW STARTED

The first three to five minutes of most interviews are used to "break the ice." Let the interviewer speak the first words, to set the tone. You will be asked a few questions of a general nature that do not require a great deal of thought. Just allow the conversation to flow, being careful to contain your answer to a moderate length—not too long or too short.

As you begin to relax and enjoy (?) yourself, the interviewer will move into topics more relevant to the college selection process, questions that delve more deeply into your personality and give you an opportunity to think on your feet. These questions will probe your background and future plans in greater depth. This should be fun if you have done some thinking about yourself and the topics that might be discussed. Answer all questions to the best of your knowledge and ability, but do not be afraid to say "I don't know." Here are a few questions that college interviewers have told me they like to ask.

—What books have you read most recently outside of school?

—If you could read the evaluation your teacher has written about you, what would it say?

—Are your standardized tests scores an accurate reflection of your true abilities?

—Are you satisfied with your academic record to date?

—What has been your most satisfying contribution to your school?

—How would you describe your two or three best friends?

—Do you have any anxieties about going to college?

—What three adjectives would you use to describe yourself?

—If you could become head of your school for a month or so, what are some of the most significant changes you would make?

—What's your favorite vegetable (you never know)?

—What do you want to learn during your college experience?

—What priorities have you established for your college experience relative to your career goals and objectives?

—If you had to convince someone who dislikes your favorite subject that it can be worthwhile, what would you say?

—What have you done in the last six months to help another person?

These are but a few examples of the types of questions interviewers regularly use to draw you out, learn about you as a person, and discover your hopes and dreams for college and the years beyond. A more complete list of questions can be found in Appendix 1.

Some interviewers will use your conversation as a chance to conduct a little market research (after all, they have a captive audience). They might ask you how you found out about the college or what you found most helpful in the college catalogue or viewbook.

TURNING THE TABLES

As soon as the interviewer feels you have had enough time to present yourself, he or she will ask if you have any questions. Here is where your preparation for the campus visit will become very apparent. If you have listed your questions on a piece of paper, ask permission to refer to that list before pulling it out of your purse or pocket.

Students who spend a week with us at the College Counselling Seminar often ask for a few good questions to use in their admission interviews. Every dean remembers a few from the past and here is a sample of my favorites.

How would you describe the relationship between your college and the local community? Answers to this query will tell the student much about the world that borders the campus and the existing opportunities for a life away from the daily academic regimen. Are jobs available? Are students welcomed in local churches and temples? Do eating establishments have any biases against college students? Do they offer college students discounts? Can students become involved with social service organizations? What about cultural or recreational outlets that supplement what is available on campus?

Is the undergraduate program compromised to advance the graduate and professional schools? Once again, this question has several subparts. Are resources being channeled away from freshman and sophomore courses and into doctoral programs? Do graduate students teach undergraduate courses? How large are the survey courses in most departments?

Why do students leave this college? Every institution has dropouts. Why do some people fail to persist until graduation? What do they discover about their choice that they did not realize before matriculating? Is there a particular personality type that might not be suited to this environment? In all fairness, keep in mind that approximately 40% of all college freshmen take longer than four years to finish their undergraduate program.

What percent of this college's total operating budget is allocated to the library? When I was asked this question a number of years ago, I went scurrying to find a financial report. (You must not expect your interviewers to know the answer to this one, but they will find the answer in due time if they're worthy of their office.) The answer says much about an institution's commitment to the maintenance of a vast repository of knowledge and the support it wishes to provide its own academic program. As a rule of thumb, anything above four percent represents a strong commitment, while less than that could be seen as a possible warning sign.

What percentage of students support the school financially after they graduate? The answer to this question reveals how satisfied students are with their academic and social experience. It will also tell you much about the financial health of the institution. After all, if alumni/ae don't support a school, why should anyone else?

What is your student/faculty ratio? This is a question with which to be careful, as a straight answer may be misleading. For example, a high number of faculty members per student might mean that en-rollment is dropping rapidly or the school is being mismanaged. What you really need to know is how many faculty members actually teach and are accessible to the students? How many primarily do research? How many are on sabbatical? What is the average size of a seminar? A lecture class?

I asked a few college admission deans to pass along some favorite questions they have received during an interview. Here are a few samples from their responses:

—What is there to do for fun?

—How extensive is the Career Counselling Center? Do you have any placement statistics?

—What percentage of your students eventually go on for graduate degrees?

—If you had to do it all over again, would you go to (your college)?

—How is your university really different from all others?

—How does college work differ from high school?

—What plans does the administration have for the college over the next several years?

—Is your location an asset or a liability?

—If you could move your campus to another setting, where would you most want it to be?

—What are the most common complaints by students at this college?

—What are the most recurring elements missing from the student body at this college?

—What in the makeup of this institution makes you come to work everyday?

—What are the strengths and weaknesses of this university?

—What are the current issues on campus?

Time will permit you to ask only a few of these plus, of course, ques-tions relative to your favorite subjects and extracurricular activities. This latter group should, if possible, be phrased in a way that first makes a statement about yourself, second indicates some familiarity with the school, and third, asks a question. For example: "I have been interested in photography for the past four years. I know your school has dark room facilities and a student run newspaper, but what other opportunities are available for photographers?"

Be sure to listen carefully to the answers rather than trying to remember or rehearse your next question. Feel free to take a few notes while your interviewer is talking, but don't try to write the answers down verbatim. A more complete list of good questions to ask appears in Appendix 2.

WRAPPING IT UP

Time permitting, your interviewer will ask if you have any further statements to make and if you are satisfied that you had an opportunity to ask all your questions. Make sure you ask your interviewer to give you an estimate of your chances for admission. This is the key item of information you want to bring back from the trip. If you like the place, is it worth your time and effort in pursuing admission from this point forward? At the conclusion of your questioning period, ask the $64,000 dollar question, "do you believe I am a realistic candidate for admission to this institution?" Then, listen carefully for the answer. Most seasoned admission interviewers will never give you a flat "no" if you are not a realistic candidate. But they will tell you if your candidacy is very strong, highly realistic, or marginal.

Finally, your interviewer will have saved a minute or two to recap the interview with your parents (either in the office or back out in the lobby) and give them an opportunity to ask any questions they might have about the institution and your prospects as a candidate. Your interviewer will then offer you a handshake and wish you the best of luck. Make sure you have written down his or her name or have a business card to include with your files. This will be your "contact person" at the college in the event that you have follow-up questions or need some idea of the status of your application. This is also the person to whom you should write your thank you note.

WHAT WILL THE INTERVIEWER SAY ABOUT THE INTERVIEW?

Immediately after you say goodbye, your interviewer will write down a few comments about the interview. Here are excerpts from reports written by actual interviewers (faculty, staff and alumni). How would you like to have some of these comments written about you?

"In the time I have been doing these interviews, I have never had one affect me as this one. She is a typical quiet, shy teenager. However, once we penetrated the surface I found a sincere young lady who wants to attend a small school because of her lack of English skills and desire to work closely with her teachers. She enjoys reading books by Sinclair Lewis and Charles Dickens. She says she enjoys the study in social life styles they present. She has established her goal in life to become a doctor. She has enjoyed working with the Red Cross and 'adopting' old people. I perceive a highly motivated person who has worked hard for what she has gotten and will work harder for what she wants. Her concern is getting assistance with her English. Beyond that she can stand on her own two feet." *(alumnus)*

"Bob appeared to be a determined, aggressive young man. He mentioned he had an uncle who attended this college. When I asked him what attracted him to us, he said that his parents thought it was a good school—it didn't appear as if he had put much thought into his reasons for wanting to attend." *(alumnus)*

"This is a classy guy. He is obviously very bright. I am impressed by his self-confidence tempered with healthy humility. He is very much his own person. His father, a physician, would really like for him to pursue a career in medicine. He has other ideas and hopes to be a lawyer. He asked well-thought-out questions regarding this college and its pre-law preparation." *(alumnus)*

"She is a young lady who impresses me as a leader and an enthusiastic active person who would serve our college well." *(alumnus)*

"She was easily the most outstanding student I spoke with today, due in part to her liveliness, her open/refreshing manner, and the diversity and depth of her interests." *(alumnus)*

"At first, Alex seemed quite nervous about the interview. She managed to relax after a time, however, and answered questions freely from that point on. She didn't display any strong academic interest, however. She mentioned our Junior Year Abroad Program, and her desire to go to France. This seemed to be more of a social rather than an academic interest. I was not overly impressed with Alex's motivation or potential and can't honestly give the Committee a strong recommendation." *(faculty)*

"I guess I thought she was trying a bit too hard to impress me with her ambition/motivation. She lacked that easy, informal comfortable element of the interview and, therefore, I don't feel like I know anything about the real Yvonne—and perhaps she doesn't either." *(staff)*

"I liked this candidate. She seems mature, positive, and enthusiastic. . .she made a comment about how exciting this year was when things she has been learning in English and history all came together." *(faculty)*

"Of the twelve people I interviewed this semester, Melissa is the best. She speaks well, with enthusiasm and animation. She thinks about the questions asked and replies thoughtfully and clearly. She will major in whatever seems most interesting (three big cheers!). She dedicated incredible amounts of time to her high school yearbook, reads novels about historical events and about the events themselves, works for her local Chamber of Commerce, and loves to write. I asked her what she would like to be able to say about herself in ten years. Her answer was: 'Not only have I learned, I have taught others as well.' That's the best answer I have received for that question." *(faculty)*

"Appearing somewhat tense at first, Michelle came across as a solid young lady during the interview. She has poise but not the relaxed confidence of sophistication. She would be 'at home' at our college. The only blemish on her good projected image was her reply to my question 'Why are you applying here?' Her answer consisted of the cliches she had rehearsed from our propaganda materials. For example, 'I would like a smaller school with a liberal arts orientation and emphasis on excellence.' Yet she is applying to large institutions and at least one state university as well.' *(faculty)*

For History Buffs

8. What school, under the presidency of Robert E. Lee, was the first to establish a school of journalism?
9. At what small mid-western school did Winston Churchill deliver his famous Iron Curtain Speech?
10. What was the first college to grant Abraham Lincoln an honorary degree?
11. What two colleges were the first in America to graduate black students?
12. What was our nation's first university? Hint: It was founded by Benjamin Franklin and included our nation's first non-sectarian college.

Sports

13. What school's rugby team was used to test the Land's End Rugby shirt?
14. At what school did the man who invented basketball coach?
15. Between what two schools was the first intercollegiate baseball game played? And what was the score?
16. What school's athletic teams have won more NCAA championships and produced more Olympic athletes than any other college or university?

4

My Final Advice on the College Interview

Before you leave for your first campus visit or interview read this chapter carefully. It will answer many of the questions you probably still have about the college interview process.

WHAT SHOULD I DO IF I NOTICE MY INTERVIEWER GROWING BORED?

The interviewer has a responsibility to show an interest in you and what you have to say. If, however, you catch your interviewer yawning or looking at his or her watch with increasing frequency, ask the interviewer a question relevant to the college. Do not just switch the topic of conversation to another of your accomplishments, in hopes the interviewer will find it more interesting.

HOW CAN I TELL IF I'M TALKING TOO MUCH?

Some people may tell you about a 90/10 rule, whereby the student does 90% of the talking, the interviewer 10%. I feel this is far too one sided. I view the college interview as a conversation between two individuals. It is a fact finding mission for both parties; a two way evaluation. Remember, you are there to look at colleges and get information not found in viewbooks, a well as be interviewed. A better "rule" would be 60/40 whereby the student does 60% of the talking.

HOW CAN I KEEP MY PARENTS FROM PUTTING SO MUCH PRESSURE ON ME?

Talk to them. Explain this is not a job interview, and you are not expected to sell yourself in quite the same way. Colleges are not looking for one perfect applicant, nor are you expected to present your entire life in thirty minutes. Also explain that the last thing you need is additional stress; what you need is their support.

WILL MY ADMISSION CHANCES BY BETTER IF MY INTERVIEW IS WITH THE DEAN OF ADMISSION RATHER THAN AN ASSOCIATE?

No. Don't worry if your interview is with someone other than the dean. All interviewers are well trained and carry equal weight in the admission process. Also, you should prepare for alumni interviews and students interviews just as you would for an interview with a member of the admission committee.

HOW CAN I SOUND SELF-CONFIDENT WITHOUT SOUNDING ARROGANT?

The key to differentiating confidence from arrogance is the student's tone of voice. It should be sort of like a good handshake—firm, but gentle. I suggest you rehearse the interview with a friend. Tape your conversation and listen to your own voice. Decide for yourself how it sounds (and whether that's the way you want it to sound).

HOW CAN I GET "REAL" INTERVIEW EXPERIENCE BEFORE I VISIT A SCHOOL?

Role playing with a friend is your best bet. If, however, you are still uneasy about the interview, I suggest you save your top choice schools for last. This way, you can practice your interview techniques with "real" admission deans, and not worry about the consequences.

WHAT SHOULD I WEAR TO THE INTERVIEW?

How you dress makes an important statement about yourself. So, in choosing what you wear, decide what sort of statement you wish to make; be sure it's not "I am a beach bum" or "I am a couch potato". Men need not wear a Wall Street suit and power tie, nor must they wear khaki pants and a navy blazer. They should, however, avoid jeans and sport shirts. For men, a nice pair of slacks with a dress shirt and a sweater is perfectly acceptable. Go lightly with the aftershave and cologne.

Like men, women do not need to wear a suit, but they should avoid slacks of all types. A dress or a skirt and blouse (or sweater) is preferred. Keep make-up and perfume to a minimum.

Do not smoke or chew gum.

Within these constraints, be certain you are comfortable. The last thing you need to worry about is whether your tie is straight or your slip is showing.

DO YOU HAVE ANY FINAL WORDS OF WISDOM?

The most important point I can make about preparing for the interview is to have a game plan. Know what you want to learn while you are on campus and what you want the people you meet to learn about you. Do not rehearse answers to the interview questions listed in this book, just use them as a guide. If you go into an interview with a script in mind, you'll find it difficult to answer anything for which you have not prepared; you will become frustrated and try to answer "your questions" anyway.

PART IV

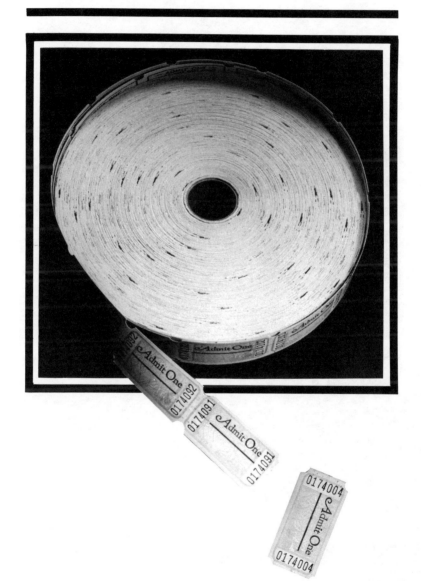

"Ten Application Forms"

5

Filling out the college application has caused many sleepless nights for high school seniors across the country. This chapter answers questions you probably have about the application and concludes with an introduction to the all important college essay.

Ten application forms, all in a line,
One asked too many questions, then there were nine.

You may wonder why some college applications ask so many questions while others are interested in little more than your name, address, and social security number. You may also wonder why no two applications ever seem to ask the same question in the same way. And, worst of all, why some schools insist on printing their applications on paper which cannot be corrected by any shade of correction fluid found on the market today.

Contrary to what you might believe, I can assure you this has not been done in an effort to ruin your senior year of high school. Let me explain.

A good college application asks as many questions as necessary for the admission committee to gain a complete understanding of each candidate. Furthermore, these schools have spent a lot of time designing their forms hoping to arrive at one that will reflect the personal characteristics of each applicant. In general, the more selective the college the more complex the application form. Selective colleges need as much information as possible about every person in their applicant pool to make admission decisions that are fair and equitable.

There is, however, good news for everyone who fears the dreaded writer's cramp. More than 100 private colleges have joined together to produce what is called the Common Application. This form is available in your high school guidance office or from the National Association of Secondary School Principals (NASSP) in Reston, Virginia. Needless to say, the Common Application is a great convenience for it allows you to fill out a single master form and make a photocopy to submit to any college in the Common Application group to which you apply. It would be most helpful if all colleges could agree to use the same form, but specific institutional needs often make this impossible. More about the Common Application in a later chapter.

To save yourself a lot of anguish, make copies of your application forms before you begin. Then, follow their directions carefully as you fill them out. Only when you are satisfied with your answers should you fill in the original.

Nine application forms none of which should wait,
One wants my senior transcript, then there were eight.

Whatever you do, don't let your grades slip during your senior year of high school! In a selective admission process, the application form is but one critical element in the decision of a faculty/staff committee. Your transcript, which represents a concise and comprehensive record of your academic performance throughout high school, is always the most important element in the admission committee's deliberations.

The reason is simple. Our goal is to admit those students who will be strong in both academic and extracurricular areas. Research shows the best predictor of academic success in college is a student's academic record in high school. In other words, the students who will probably get the best grades in college are the ones who had the best grades in high school. If you feel the need to explain a bad grade, you should do so in a separate letter.

Your secondary school transcript will also tell the reader something about the quality of your preparation for college. The courses you select say as much as the grades you receive about your desire to make the most of your academic opportunities. As you select your courses, remember, if you do not challenge yourself in high school, why should an admission committee think you will challenge yourself in college? In other words, is your 4.0 grade point average a result of advanced placement hopscotch or advanced placement English, Math, and Chemistry?

Next, the admission committee believes your most recent grades and courses are the best reflection of your readiness for college. They carefully scrutinize your first semester senior year transcript, then look at your 11th grade record. They are less rigorous in their study of your 10th grade and 9th grade performance. In other words, it is possible to have a bad freshman or sophomore year and recover in time to show selective colleges you are indeed ready for a more demanding experience. Again I emphasize the importance of maintaining a challenging academic program throughout your senior year. As much as you may feel you deserve it, your final year of high school is not the time to slack off (and I assure you, good college admission officers know when students slack off. Whether their knowledge comes from weighted transcripts or conversations with teachers and counselors, these people know which courses are hard and which ones are easy).

Finally, if you must take a year off before college, do so after your senior year. Most selective colleges will allow admitted candidates to defer entrance for up to one year.

Eight application forms, I need help from heaven,
One asked for Board scores, then there were seven.

The use of standardized tests like the SAT and the ACT has become a major issue in higher education during the eighties. To quote from

Robert and Anna Leider's book, *Don't Miss Out,* "The SAT has become a national industry. The money spent on designing tests, administering tests, scoring tests, taking tests, teaching tests, coaching tests, disseminating test results, selling the names and scores of test takers to eager college recruiters, interpreting scores, analyzing scores, publicizing scores, and writing about the test, pro and con, places the SAT somewhat below automobiles, but far ahead of the value of the horseradish crop as a contributor to our gross national product...."

The result of all this attention has been the acknowledgement that standardized tests do not measure creativity. They do not measure intelligence. They do not measure motivation. And therefore, they should not be used to predict academic success. Nevertheless, tests continue to play an important role in the admission process as exactly that—a predictor of how a student might do in college. The reason is simple. There is such great variation among high schools in the quality of teaching, the quality of courses offered, the quality of textbooks, and the consistency of grading policies that admission committees perceive SAT/ACT scores as a common denominator. The SAT or ACT is the same test whether it is taken in Paris or Peoria. It is an international exam.

While standardized tests scores are not as important as your high school transcript, they are a convenient screening device for admission committees faced with thousands of applications for only a few remaining spots, and until a more equitable way of measuring a student's ability is developed, the SAT and ACT will continue to play a role in the admission decision. Note: You are responsible for having the testing agency send an official copy of your test scores to each school to which you apply. The admission committee might not accept the scores as reported on your high school transcript.

Seven application forms, quite a heady mix,
One needed Dean's approval, then there were six.

Asking a teacher for a recommendation has filled many a high school student with anxiety. How can you be certain the person you ask will do a good job? What happens if the person you ask only gave you a passing grade so you'd never enroll in that class again?

If the college requires recommendations from one or more teachers, you should select a person (1) who knows you well and (2) who is apt to write a first-rate recommendation about you as a scholar and a person. Don't automatically select the most popular teacher in school. Popularity might mean that teacher has so many recommendations to write that the quality of those recommendations will be diluted. Think how would you feel about writing a recommendation for every college bound member of the senior class... Nor should you automatically select the teacher from whom you received your highest grades. Instead, think about the teacher for whom you made the greatest progress. That would be the person who could speak to your willingness to work hard, overcome learning barriers, and grow in the process. These are the qualities of an ideal candidate for college admission.

As for your fears that a bad recommendation will be written, relax. If the teacher does not feel qualified to write a recommendation for you, or does not want to write a recommendation for you, he or she will tell you so.

Students often despair when a letter of recommendation is required from their high school guidance counselor because in many instances their counselor doesn't even know their name (or if they do, it's because the student has been in some kind of trouble—not the kind of thing you want mentioned in a recommendation). The solution—make an effort to get to know your counselor. To do this you don't have to join the ranks of the "discipline problems." Just make an appointment to talk. Tell your counselor about your plan, and listen to any advice that is given. When it does come time for your counselor to write the high school's official recommendation, feel free to provide supporting material. A resume is very helpful.

Even though they may not be requested, feel free to request letters from other people who know you well. Is there an athletic coach who knows you as a team player? a drama teacher who could speak of your artistic flare? or a community leader who might describe your involvement with the local literacy campaign?

61

Please allow everyone plenty of time to write your recommendations. This way, they are less apt to be rushed form letters, and more likely to be considered evaluations of your abilities and qualifications. It's also common courtesy.

The question of whether or not to waive your right to read your recommendations is a personal one. Most students do so, but it is your choice and is not likely to affect the content of the recommendation. An admission committee, however, may see failure to waive your right as an indication of insecurity.

Six application forms, time to come alive,
One had an early deadline, then there were five.

Don't think of application deadlines as the date when you have to do something. Instead, set your dates at least two weeks earlier. This way you'll avoid paying Federal Express a small fortune for their faster than the speed of light delivery service (remember, you're already paying many dollars in application fees). Keep a chart which lists each school and its deadlines. Don't forget schools often have separate deadlines for test scores and financial aid forms.

Generally, you will find two basic admission calendars: "rolling" and "precipice." In the rolling admission process, applications are reviewed as soon as they are complete and admission decisions are made as soon as possible. Some rolling admissions require a rolling response, i.e., accepted students have a relatively short period of time in which to decide whether or not to enroll. Also, in the rolling process, the first to apply probably have a better chance of gaining admission since there are more places available in the freshman class.

In the precipice admission process, all applications that arrive before a final deadline are gathered and all candidates are notified of acceptance/rejection on one date (e.g., January 15 application deadline; April 1 notification date). These schools usually adhere to the National Candidates Reply Date of May 1. By this day you must decide which college to attend and make a non-refundable tuition and room reservation deposit. While colleges prefer to see applications mailed as soon as possible (this helps the people who must do all the paperwork), you get no special reward for applying prior to the final deadline. You do, however, face severe penalties for missing it (like not being considered for admission, no matter how outstanding your credentials).

Early Decision is a process that allows students who have made a clear first-choice to apply before the regular application deadline and receive an Early Evaluation of their chances (perhaps an offer of admission) in the fall of their senior year. Early Decision eliminates the necessity of filing multiple applications and the anxiety of waiting until spring for admission decisions to arrive. Often schools will assume Early Decision candidates are committed to attending and thus accept a greater percentage of those who apply Early Decision than of those who apply during the regular admission season. Each college, however, has its own philosophy regarding admission standards for those who apply Early Decision, and this information should be obtained from every college near the top of your list.

Five application forms, oh they're such a chore,
One lacked space for "other interests," then there were four.

The record of your extracurricular activities tells a lot about you as a person. Are you active? Do you like to be busy? Do you enjoy events that involve cooperation among people? Are you a "team player" in the sense that you enjoy working with a group in pursuit of common goals? Are you a leader? No one activity is most highly prized by admission officers. There is a tendency to look for depth more than breadth in a list of activities, as this usually makes for a better college student. For example, a deep commitment to one or two school activities will probably look better than a smorgasbord of memberships in loosely organized clubs. The Presidency of Apathy International does not impress a committee. Furthermore, a deep commitment to one or two activities is also better for your personal growth—regardless of the admission committee.

When filling out this part of the application, be careful not to just list activities. Within the alloted space, explain why each activity is important, and what you have learned as a result. Also, remember to include work experience (even if it's not specifically requested), especially if your work has prevented you from taking part in the usual variety of after-school events.

Finally, athletes might want to send a separate letter to the coach of their sport at the college. They should include newspaper clippings, team records, and personal statistics. Similarly, those with an interest in music should send tapes of a performance and aspiring artists should send slides of their work (both to the admission committee and the chairperson of the appropriate department).

Four application forms, all addressed to me,
One came from "Nowhere State," then there were three.

Newspaper headlines this past fall carried conflicting stories. One day you read that selective colleges are no longer selective, that students can do the choosing. Declining school populations and aggressive recruitment activities seem to legitimize this claim. The very next day, in the same paper, even in the same column, you read that applications are up at colleges and universities across the country by as much as 20%. Schools are more selective than ever. So what's a person to believe?

The most soundly based explanation deals with the anxieties of today's college age generation. Simply put, high school students are very worried about gaining admission to a reputable school, and file more and more applications to guard against the unlikely possibility they will not be admitted anywhere. At $20 to $50 a crack, applying to fifteen colleges is an expensive and time consuming proposition which can and should be avoided.

I advise you to spend some of that application-writing time reading about colleges and meeting with their representatives to learn more about programs, policies, and your chances of gaining admission.

Ideally, students should never apply to more than five schools with at least one "insurance policy" in that group. If more decisions were made before applying, there would be benefits to all. Not only would it leave you more time to enjoy your winter break, but it would greatly relieve hundreds (thousands?) of bleary-eyed admission deans who must stay up all hours of the night digging into a pile of applications that grows higher with each passing year.

If financial assistance must be an important factor in your ultimate college choice, you should request information about financial aid at the same time you request an application form. Find out what percentage of people who need assistance actually get assistance, and what the average award size is. Also find out how awards are made. If your own family circumstances are somewhat unique or complicated and a particular college is reluctant to be flexible in evaluating your special circumstances, you may find yourself unable to attend such a college even if your application is approved.

I advise you, however, not to base your college selection process on the cost of the school. Your number one priority should be getting into the best school for you. Then worry about the finances. Reading a book like *Don't Miss Out* (from Octameron) will provide answers to your money woes.

Three application forms, all overdue,
One wants a photograph, then there were two.

So you don't think you're photogenic? The picture-while-you-wait booth at the drugstore wasn't working? Well, colleges can no longer require that a photograph be attached to the application form. Many students choose to, because they believe their photo is a statement about themselves and the college has encouraged them to enclose or attach any information that will give the selection committee a better "picture" of their qualifications. One of my favorites was a swimmer who sent us her picture in the form of a baseball card. On the reverse side we found her "statistics". . . her SAT scores, her GPA, her class rank, her height and weight, her hobbies, and her fastest freestyle times. "Big League Cards" in New Jersey will print these for you. Other people have sent entire photo albums, some have put their photo on the cover of magazine. The decision, however, is yours. The absence of anything not required for admission will never be used to discriminate against a candidate. In other words, additional information, if used at all, will only be used in a positive manner.

Two application forms, the battle's half the fun,
One cost fifty bucks to process, now there's only one.

Colleges strongly believe that no qualified and deserving person should ever be denied the opportunity to apply or enroll at their institutions because of financial limitations. With this in mind, the application fee (which currently ranges from $10-$50) will be waived provided the candidate attaches a letter from a school official stating the fee will be a financial hardship on the applicant and the applicant's family. Most admission committees will not be aware that an application fee has been waived as they review the credentials of a candidate. Those that do will in no way allow the fee waiver to have a negative impact on the decision unless, of course, they have reason to suspect the applicant has not been honest about family financial circumstances in requesting the waiver.

One application form, at last I'm nearly done,
Just the essay left to write and then there was none.

To appreciate fully the importance of the essay in an admission committee's decision, I must summarize some of the foregoing discussion.

The college admission process focuses first on secondary school academic performance and the results of standardized tests. It then looks at one's personal characteristics as evidenced by recommendations, the interview and the application form. This is not meant to imply the application and the personal side of the essay question are less important. In fact, most applicants to selective colleges are qualified for admission. That is to say their secondary school transcripts and SAT/ACT results compare favorably with the majority of students already enrolled at the school. How then do the deans make their decisions? More often than not, they focus on this second category—personal qualities. In fact, in most instances, the more selective the college, the more important personal qualities are in the selection process. And where are these qualities best found? In the essay. In short, at the highest and finest level, the admission process becomes highly subjective with human beings engaged in the process of evaluating other human beings on human terms.

If this is a worrisome thought or if it causes you to ponder what might be perceived as a whimsical, capricious, even unfair way of making decisions, remember, so is life. Human performance is extremely difficult to quantify, categorize or predict. Although we must continue to attempt to be as fair and objective as we possibly can, the reality of the college selection process very much resembles the evaluations that will be made of you and your performance throughout your lifetime.

But, it is time to stop all this scary talk and say something more comforting. The good thing about the college application is that it offers you the opportunity to assume control of the flow of information between you and the colleges. It is here that you can pop up and show the college selection committee you are more than just a list of courses or grades on a transcript or the numbers that result from a three-hour multiple choice examination. Most application forms also offer you the opportunity to send something else, an attachment which may demonstrate your creative ability in areas such as art, photography, or music. Photographic essays, an art portfolio, or slides, or a music tape are frequently mailed to colleges in the hopes of enhancing a candidates's personal evaluation. Each of these highlights you and tells the college something about you that is unobtainable in any other way.

When you think about it, it is only fair you get the chance to choose how you wish to be portrayed. After all, most of what you are able to learn about colleges is packaged for you by the colleges themselves. They design the catalogues, the viewbooks, and the leaflets and decide what information to give you.

Finally, this brings us to the essays, which are without question, the most difficult and the most important element over which you have control in the admission process. A well written essay will differentiate the truly exciting student from the merely good one, and tip the scale in your favor in the most difficult of decisions faced by an admission committee.

I am always puzzled by the number of applicants to selective colleges who do less than a top-notch job in answering the essay questions. Most essays are so tedious and so dry that they conjure up a tedious and dry personality. Or worse, suggest the applicants have nothing of interest to say about themselves, their values, their opinions about life, or their optimism for the college years and beyond. The application essays are the most misunderstood and underestimated elements in the process of applying to college. I hope to remedy that in the remaining parts of this book.

Culture

17. What was the first American University to offer an academic degree in ballet?
18. At what school did Meryl Streep begin her commencement address by singing Qué Será Será?
19. From what school did the gemologist who found the engagement ring Richard Burton gave Elizabeth Taylor graduate?
20. At what school can you play the original Moog Synthesizer used to record the album Switched On Bach?

Campus Hotspots

21. At what school can you find "The Bald Spot?"
22. What school boasts the world's largest student union?
23. What student union at what school sells three tons of fudge annually AND houses a family of lizards?
24. What school's setting did Thoreau say was at least as good as one well-endowed professorship?
25. What school is guarded day and night by a pride of concrete dinosaurs?

PART V

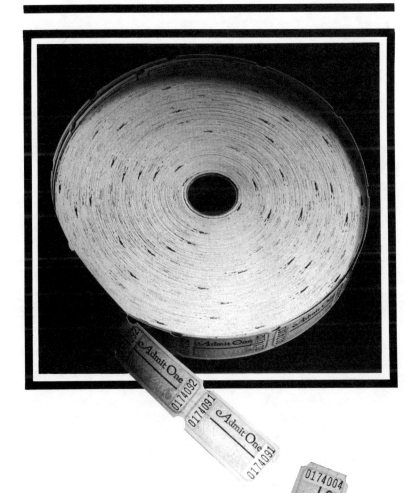

6

The Essay—What are They Looking For?

The answer to this perplexing question begins with a thorough study of the directions provided by the college and a complete understanding of the questions or statements presented. Pay particular attention to directions regarding length, style, and format. If the intended readers want it to be typed or printed, make sure you type or print. Although there is no ideal length for a college essay, beware of the extremes, i.e., too long or too brief. Give yourself enough time to cover the subject but don't indulge in overkill.

I have never seen a college application essay question, no matter how it was worded, that did not ask the same basic thing—who are you, and what makes you different from all of those other qualified applicants we must consider? In other words, the essay gives you an opportunity to demonstrate those qualities which make you unique. Three of the most common questions are "Describe a personally satisfying experience," "What are your most significant academic interests?" and "Explain how you think our college will help you grow." All of these questions ask you to shed some light on your values, opinions, and talents. They require you to take some time to think about what has happened to you personally and why certain subjects have always been your favorites. They offer you the chance to demonstrate why you are someone special. The college expects no single answer. Instead, think of the essay as your chance to introduce yourself to the college. What would you like it to know about you that is not found in transcripts, test scores, or even a personal interview. This is no easy feat because we usually hide our true selves because of social peer pressure to conform. After spending seventeen years of your life avoiding the description "weird", you may find the essay question to be difficult because you must think about all of the characteristics that make you different from your friends, that is, a unique human being. Keep in mind your friends will never read the essay unless you show it to them, and the college application will never become a public document. So you have great freedom and no reason not to reach deep within yourself and bring out the person you have kept under wraps for so long.

The typical admission committee reader is looking at your finished product on three levels. At the lowest level, they skim your words to see if you can write. Your spelling, grammar, syntax, and usage must all be absolutely perfect. This implies the need for a proofreader because all of us make mistakes that don't necessarily jump off the page but are quickly apparent to another reader. Even professional writers do not edit their own work. Your high school English teacher might be a good person to read your essay, and don't forget Mom or Dad, especially if they do a lot of writing in their daily work.

If you are proofing your own work, here are two suggestions. One. Use a ruler or a blank sheet of paper to cover the lines beneath the one you are reading. This will keep your eyes more focussed. Two. Read your essay backwords. This will prevent you from skimming the text and force you to look carefully at each individual word. Whatever method you use, read the essay aloud and keep a dictionary close at hand.

At the second level, they consider the content of your answer. Here the reader is concerned with the logic of your argument and your ability to say something of substance in a relatively economical and effective manner. Here is where overly long and redundant essays can seriously penalize the writer. Having something interesting to say makes your task much easier so make sure you have taken the time to develop sentiments or ideas that are interesting to read.

At the final and most important level, the reader is hoping to see something creative. What better way to express your individuality than a story, perhaps a brief dialogue, or an attempt at humor? Poetry is appropriate for open-ended questions but extremely difficult to write if the question is somewhat specific. Creative work brings an element of risk to your essay. What if they won't think it's funny? Or sad? Or if they miss the point? Or they think you're obnoxious? Nevertheless, your willingness to take a risk is particularly important because so many of today's young people seem conservative and unwilling to take chances. Most essays I read these days lack the creative element because most students simply don't take the "river boat gambler" approach to the process. Please understand I am not suggesting you "throw caution to the wind." But those who take any risk at all will quickly stand out from today's applicant pool and enhance their candidacy. A good rule of thumb is that the risk one takes should be inversely related to the perceived chances for admission. In other words, the greater your certainty of being accepted, the less risk you need to take with your essays.

Of course, college admission officers want to read essays that are fresh, upbeat, and lively. We would like each answer to offer us a picture of the candidate that just isn't visible in a list of courses and grades or the numbers resulting from a three-hour multiple choice examination. We want to "see" the writer as someone who stands alone on the master grid of applicants to our institution, someone we'd like to get to know better.

When you think about it, you must sell yourself to a college in much the same way a college must sell itself to you. And the whole process is very similar to what goes on in the boardrooms of the nation's largest corporations every day. Any company that markets a product is continually faced with the problem of positioning itself on a grid with rival companies and their seemingly similar products. The company must find some way to make its product stand out so the consumer perceives it to be different, unique, better. Likewise, colleges must spend time determining how it is they differ from other colleges, and then, how to convince you, the consumer, that that difference makes them a better place to be. When their college representatives tell high school students that their college is unique, they are telling the truth. No two colleges are the same. And each can position itself as a unique institution. College viewbooks and pamphlets herald the unique characteristics of their particular institution, and phrases such as "a special place" are not uncommon, nor are they untrue.

Now you see how it works with you the student. There has never been anyone who is just like you. We college admission officers know that, but we leave it to you to tell us how you are special. Reading application essays is great fun because so many applicants put so much effort into their descriptive paragraphs. Writing them should be just as enjoyable. In selective college admission, applicants who fail to understand the importance of the essays and don't put forth the necessary effort, seriously jeopardize their chance to position themselves and lose the opportunity to enhance their academic credentials in the competition for a limited number of great opportunities. Think of it this way, where would your favorite cola or fast food chain be without well thought out advertising campaigns?

The Student Body

26. What college was founded in a room over a shoestore as a school of penmanship?
27. What school was the first to be established as a coeducational institution?
28. What New England men's college was the first to go coed?
29. What is the only Jewish-sponsored, nonsectarian institution of higher learning in the United States?
30. From what college did Rutherford B. Hayes and Paul Newman graduate?
31. What school ranks first in its percentage of alumni listed in Who's Who in America?

A Conversation with the Dean

The following "conversation" summarizes some of my best advice concerning the college essay. If you feel there are some questions I have not answered, please send them to me via my publisher, Octameron Associates, PO Box 3437, Alexandria, VA 22302, and I will address them in the next edition of this publication.

Candidate:

I'm stuck on these college essays! I haven't had this serious a case of writer's block since my Sixth grade "What I did on my summer vacation" essay.

Dean:

Welcome to the club. Remember—writing the essay is supposed to be a difficult task. Otherwise, everyone would breeze right through it and no one would gain an advantage in the process of selection. Think of this as your big chance to rise above the crowd.

Candidate:

Can you at least help me get started; give me a clue as to what you deans are looking for? Is this supposed to be a soap opera version of my life story, or a treatise on the meaning of life?

Dean:

We want to meet the real you—someone other than a grade point average, an SAT score, and a class rank—a living, breathing human being who has both strengths and weaknesses. It is just as important for us to know what you think needs improvement in yourself as it is for us to know how you hope to strengthen our campus. Seriously, if you are already perfect, what can our college possibly do for you?

Candidate:

Why am I having such a hard time finding the real me?

Dean:

Like most of us, you spend a lot of time trying to be like everyone else, conforming to peer pressures. "Finding yourself" is a life-long (and rewarding) battle, and now is a good time to start. You need only stop and ask yourself "How am I different from my friends and other classmates?"

Candidate:

What if I say the wrong thing?

Dean:

There are no right and wrong answers to a college essay question. No one in an admission office reading applicants' folders wants to think the freshman class will be filled by a bunch of docile conformists. No one has a particular personality trait he or she wants to purge from the student body. So you see, you can't lose—if you are honest about yourself.

Candidate:

What do you mean "honest"?

Dean:

I mean realistic about who you are and who you are not. Believe me, we can spot "phony" all the way across a room full of folders, sort of like Santa knowing who's been good and who's been bad. We also know when someone else (especially a parent) is responsible for the answers. Write the essays yourself and never allow yourself to be misrepresented by anyone, including yourself.

Candidate:

How do I get started?

Dean:

Get off by yourself and take stock of who you are. How did you get to this point in your life? What are your values? How were they acquired? Parents? Heroes? Friends? Teachers? Have they changed in recent years? Can you recall an event buried in your brain that typifies how you feel about the topic presented in the essay question? Have you met a particular person or read a book that has had a profound impact on your values and opinions? What has been the greatest tragedy of your life or what has been the biggest void you have ever felt? How about your happiest moment or your greatest thrill? (I used superlatives for emphasis. You may have more than one response to each question.)

Candidate:

Do I have to worry that my answers will ever come back to haunt me? Will I one day find them published in a book like this?

Dean:

Of course not. The admission process is a relatively private one and the answers you provide are meant specifically to assist the readers in their evaluation of your record. Is this institution the place for you to continue your growth and development? Nothing you say on an application form can ever come back to haunt you as long as it is a truthful representation of who you are at that point in time. It is only a snapshot, not a long-running motion picture.

Candidate:

How long should the essay be?

Dean:

Only as long as necessary to make your point. Avoid overly verbose responses. Say your piece as concisely and economically as possible and don't worry about the length (unless, of course, the application requests a specific length; then, follow those instructions exactly).

Candidate:

What are some of the big mistakes people make?

Dean:

For one, they frequently start writing their answer before they have carefully read the question and all of the directions provided. Try to imagine how you would react, as a college selection committee member, to an answer written by someone who obviously had not read (or understood) the question or the directions. Is this the kind of student you want at your college? No. At best, it indicates carelessness. Second, a number of people mistakenly attempt to stretch their vocabulary by using words with which they are not entirely comfortable. They forget that some of the best writing of all time has been done in one and two syllables (think of the poetry of Ogden Nash and Dr. Seuss), so please don't worry about using big words in an application essay. Another common mistake is the failure to check spelling. As long as one proofreader remains in this world, you have no excuse for sending in an application with misspelled words or typographical errors.

Candidate:

Why do some colleges insist on having their own applications and essay questions? I may be able to write one or two essays, but dozens. . . .?

Dean:

We need to vary the questions to make certain we do not fall into a rut. You only have to write a few answers. We have to read thousands, and when multiplied over the years, essays can become quite monotonous. We need to "rearrange the furniture" to keep our minds fresh and open to new insights from new applicants each year. Of course colleges also like to have their own essay questions because they believe their application form makes a statement about them and the unique properties of their selection process.

Candidate:

Does this mean colleges that belong to the Common Application Agreement do not think of themselves as unique?

Dean:

Absolutely not. The colleges in the Common Application group have made a great sacrifice for the benefit of you the candidate. They have given up the right to have their own application questions to make it possible for you to apply to a broader range of colleges without undue effort. This means, of course, your work on the Common Application can and should be absolutely first-rate. After all, with but one application form, you are able to be considered for admission to a number of very fine institutions. There is no excuse for a mistake, or a less than terrific essay. The Common Application is a good idea that is supported by all of those institutions who belong to the group. Membership in that group means the colleges are very interested in you personally and in making your application to college as painless as humanly possible.

Candidate:

Can I change anything after my application has been mailed? You never know, I may win the Nobel prize...

Dean:

Of course. If you win the Nobel prize, we certainly want to know about it. You should, however, make certain your original answers are thoroughly considered, and only make changes if you believe they will have a significant impact on our admission decision. Just clearly identify yourself as a previous applicant and the author of any additional work submitted.

8

General Guidelines for Writing the Essay

Everything you have ever learned about good writing applies to the task of writing strong, lucid college application essays. Before beginning, you might want to pick up a copy of *The Elements of Style* by William Strunk, Jr. and E.B. White. Mr. Strunk was an English professor at Cornell University who originally printed this little book privately as a text for his writing course. Fifty years later, his words are still invaluable.

ORGANIZING YOUR THOUGHTS

Mr. Strunk has sage advice on organizing and composing your thoughts. "Writing, to be effective, must follow closely the thoughts of the writer, but not necessarily in the order in which those thoughts occur." *(The Elements of Style,* 1972, p. 10) Your essay should have three parts; an introduction to the subject, the subject, and a review of your main points. You can organize your paragraphs in a similar fashion. Each should have a topic sentence to hold the paragraph together or a transitional sentence to connect the paragraph to previous narration; a middle in which you provide the details of your argument; and a conclusion in which you summarize your main points.

Before you begin to write, make a list of possible topics. I hesitate to recommend one for fear everyone who reads this book will use it. After you have decided on a topic, turn it into a thesis. For instance "My life as a Werewolf" might become "Discovering I was a Werewolf taught me not to judge people by their appearance." Next, outline three or four examples that will prove your thesis. And finally, sum up your essay in a concluding paragraph.

If the topic and situation permit, you can now take this formula and be creative. Start with an attention getting first line, and then make your main point. For instance: A full moon means only one thing; time for a new pedicure and flea collar. Since becoming a werewolf...

OMIT NEEDLESS WORDS

One of Strunk's most important rules is "Omit Needless Words". This is what he says: "Vigorous writing is concise. A sentence should contain no unnecessary words, a paragraph no unnecessary sentences for the same reason that a drawing should have no unnecessary lines and a machine no unnecessary parts. This requires not that the writer make all his sentences short, or that he avoid all detail and treat his subjects only in outline, but that every word tell." *(The Elements of Style,* 1972, p. 17) What are some of his other suggestions? Keep your style simple, vary the length of your sentences (but avoid run-ons), and use the active voice whenever possible.

OTHER GUIDELINES

As a writer of an application essay, you are given the luxury of almost unlimited time, and for good reason. The delivery of a clear and concise personal snapshot in verbal form should be a difficult and time consuming task. It should also be fun, if one begins the process early and takes the time necessary to do a first-rate job.

The writing should be your own—your ideas, your words, and your style of expression. Do not plagiarize. Do not let someone else write for you. Having said this, remember that very few of us who depend upon effective communications in our daily jobs would ever consider a writing job finished that had not been read, reread, and even proofread by someone we trust to read critically. My suggestion. Write a first draft. Let it sit for a few days. Then read it out loud, and listen to yourself. How does it sound? Does it flow easily, or does it seem awkward, stilted? After you are satisfied with your work, then give it to someone else to read. Remember, what seems logical to you, may not to someone else.

Pay special attention to directions and do not exceed any limits placed by the institutions to whom the application will be sent. If space beyond that which is provided to answer a question is necessary, use additional paper so long as the institution does not specifically prohibit it in the directions which accompany the application. If your essay cannot exceed the space provided, trace that space onto a scrap sheet of paper. Then, keep writing, editing, and retyping until your sentences fit. Remember, when your space is limited, it is important to make every word count. Even if you are an accomplished calligrapher, you should type your answers. A professional typist is usually allowed as long as that person does not take the liberty of editing your work. The advent of the word processor has made proofing and self-editing much easier, but so many of the printers currently available do not make a bold, clear, easy to read impression. Put yourself in the place of someone reading thousands of essays. Remember how much more impressive your writing will seem if it is clearly visible to tired eyes.

Above all else, your writing should be crisp and positive and energized. It should attract the reader by its freshness and the interesting nature of its substance. It should say in so many words "Look at me! I am fresh and exciting and creative and like no other candidate you have met in your entire career." This is the approach that will make a difference.

Sample Essay Questions

As I mentioned earlier, all college applications ask the same basic question—who are you, and what makes you different from all those other qualified applicants we must consider? Most applications, however, have their own way of asking for this information. Some schools feel general questions allow students greater freedom to express themselves, and consequently, lead to more reflective essays. Other schools feel specific questions are necessary to unveil the person behind the transcript and test scores. Below you will find some of the more creative wordings used by colleges and universities in the past.

1. Describe the social atmosphere at your school and tell how you fit in. (Carleton)

2. Write a letter to your new college roommate introducing yourself and describing your background. (Carleton)

3. Ask and answer the one important question which you wish we had asked. (Carleton)

4. Please write about an intellectual, social, political, or personal issue you feel is important. (Cornell)

5. If you were to describe yourself by a quotation, what would that quotation be? (Dartmouth)

6. Given the authority to establish a holiday, what would you choose to commemorate? (Stanford)

7. Suppose you had the opportunity to spend a day with anyone. With whom would it be and how would you spend your time? (Stanford)

8. Name three things you'd carry to safety if your home was burning, and explain why you chose them. (Stanford)

9. Imagine the year is 1881. You may expect to live another 35 years. What person would you most want to know well during that time? For what reasons? (Swarthmore)

10. Identify a person who has had a significant influence on you, and describe that influence. (Wesleyan)

11. Share with us what other (Wesleyan) students would learn from you both inside and outside the classroom. (Wesleyan)

Campus Traditions

32. At what school was the nation's first social sorority founded?
33. At what school can you find the Chung Mungs, Bum Chums, Paint and Patches, Aints and Asses, The Sweet Tones, and The Earphones?
34. At what school can you participate in Devil-Goat Day?
35. What school's students hosted the World's first indoor beach party? Ate the first banana split? Celebrated a 100-hour April-Fool-Weekend? Hint, it's located in "Mr. Rogers" real home town neighborhood.

10
Sample Essays

Writing about yourself is difficult. We all are raised to be humble and modest, to play down our achievements. But your mission in writing this essay is clear: To sell yourself to a college, to gain admission. No matter how the question is written, it asks you to introduce yourself as a person with unique "product attributes." Why should you be selected over so many other qualified and deserving candidates? Remember, selling anything involves what the business world calls "product positioning." So, you must set yourself apart from others in the applicant pool. Answers to the following questions will get you started. Who are you? What do you like? What are your skills? What do you value? What do you look for in a friend? Is there something someone once said to you that you have never forgotten? What does this tell others about you? How would your friends describe you? Has there been a special teacher who has changed your way of looking at life—who has truly inspired you? What made him/her so special? How did you change?

As you answer these questions, and as you write your essay, remember to be specific, and go beyond a simple narration of events. In other words, don't stop with who, what, and where, get to the how and the why.

Let's turn now to some examples of essays that were written in support of college applications. Most of these examples will be positive but first let's look at some "Don'ts".

Here's an example of someone who wrote to answer the question, "What are your most significant academic interests?"

> I enjoy history and sociology. History is fascinating because there is something you have not learned yet. Sociology deals with people and how they interact.

This kind of answer fails to reveal anything about the author as a person.

––––––––

Here's one that was written in the open-ended section of the college application. Not only is it carelessly composed and full of misspelled words, but it is cliched and lacking in substance:

> "I would very deeply like for you, Rhinestone, to take my application into very deep thought and consideration, for I would like to further my education to the best of my knowledge. And I feel Rhinestone is the college best suited for my needs. Rhinestone is just an all around good school. I was down talking to Mr. Smith the Varsity Baseball coach, and he took me a tour of the school, I loved it. It defintly is a nice and beutiful school. The surroundings, climate and just the way the people and Mr. Smith was, really extremely impressed me. And like I said my major is going to be Law, and I feel you are the best college for my major. (By the way it is a 6 your drive from my house to the college, so this should say a little something about how deeply interested I am in you college.)
>
> "And like my principal said, I am a very dedicated and respectful young man. I do not mean to be bragging or bosting, but I feel it is the truth. I respect people for what they

are and for what they stand for. And I try my best not to bring any harm or danger to anybody or anything, just because I love life, I try and make every day count, because 'What you do today is important because you are exchanging a day of your life for it.'

"I do not know what else to say other than I would very much like to attend your college, I mean this from the bottom of my heart. Because like I said I feel it is the best college to further my education to the best of my knowledge.

"P.S. Because I am handing my application in at this time or should I say near the deadline, does not mean a thing. I was not contacted or aware of what kind of college Rhinestone really is. But now I know what kind of college Rhinestone really is and I would defintly like to attend your college.

"Thank You very much."

———————

And here is one more example of how a person failed to use the opportunity to draw a clear and comprehensive picture of himself:

I would like to explain a little of myself in this section. I feel this is important. In most instances, one does not have the chance to speak of one's self. Most allow cold, hard, impersonal fact to stand for their being. I am glad this is an exception to that rule.

While growing up, my life has been through many instances in which I had to learn to cope or be left in the cold. While still a pre-teen the illness of my father forced great mental reponsabilities upon me. I was forced to cope with being located in one area for a long period of time. This, being from a military family, was a great shock. Also, being the youngest of three, I had to go through this alone as for the other two were away at school. This meant going through a life of trial-error basis which extended through my high school career. Finally reaching college level, I must once again step out on my own. I would like to do this by going to your school.

Thank you.

This might have been an interesting essay but the reader was constantly distracted by grammatical and typographical errors. In addition, the first paragraph is so wordy it puts off any reader who is making a sincere attempt to take some measure of the writer.

What does this next essay tell you about this writer?

An experience which resulted in personal satisfaction is something I cannot seem to recall at the present time. I do not remember one distinct personally satisfying experience. Satisfaction may be a gradual thing in my case. Then again, it may not be. This may be a problem in need of a solution.

Perhaps the writer did not understand the question or, worse yet, he lacked the time and effort necessary to really think about a personally satisfying experience. It is difficult for me to believe that the writer was truly unable to recall a personally satisfying experience or that satisfaction may be a gradual thing in his case. What would an essay like this do to your college chances?

Read this next essay as if you are a college admission dean. What suggestions would you use to make it more interesting?

I have found the death of my grandmother has had a significant effect on my life. It drove home the fact that no one is perfect for we all have that fatal flaw. It caused me to look to my future and make a decision as to what I shall do with myself. At this moment I am pursuing a goal which I have set. That goal is what I came up with after my grandmother's death and I shall pursue it to the best of my ability and college is a step toward that goal.

First, the sentences are hopelessly long and tiring. Also, several important questions remain unanswered. Each sentence could be the beginning of its own paragraph. For example, how did reality dawn upon him? What is his goal? How will college be the major step he hopes it will be?

Sometimes, you might not be in the right frame of mind to write an essay. At least that's what this offering suggests.

> No single person or event has had that tremendous an impact on my life. For, in all truth, my life has more or less blended itself into one quiet day of existence after another. Which, is for the largest part, the reason I wish to go to college and hopefully, in doing so, remove myself from this monotonous routine. I do not consider myself an inactive nor apathetic a person toward events, in fact, I am quite easily interested in the slightest of enterprises. Yet, each seems after its conclusion, to fade into a still life. Soon, thereafter, my life seems to return itself back to the same state of ennui with which it perpetuates itself in hopeless constant boredom.

Once you read beyond the distractions of poor punctuation, you sense this person might have been having a bad day. If your mood is dull or flat, it will definitely be reflected in your writing. This writer should have walked away and tried again on a sunnier day.

This enterprising applicant thought he had a great idea.

> You could call the place I work and ask how I work. The number is 123-456-7890. I think they will tell you a lot about me. I have been working there for a long time and they know me very well.

No, the college did not make the call. A letter of recommendation from the employer would have been a better way of handling the situation.

Now let's turn our attention to some interesting examples that are fun to read and truly insightful as well. Notice how this author grabs the reader's attention with the very first words:

'Ball!' shouted the umpire. I was thunderstruck; the pitch was belt-high, down the middle of the plate. The umpire later told me he had never seen the ball because he was so astonished to see a left-handed softball pitcher. That such a thing should happen to a five-year All-Star pitcher with State and Regional tournament experience was unbelievable.

This is just another example of discrimination against left-handed people. The very word 'left' has negative connotations: leftover, left out, left-handed compliment, left-footed, and out in left field. The French word *gauche* means 'left' but connotes 'lacking in social graces.' Southpaws are continually having to adapt to a right-handed world. Doors open the wrong way for lefties, fold-hiding zippers are awkward for them to unzip, cradled telephones are on the wrong side, and the car ignitions and gearshifts are in the wrong places. Manufacturers of playing cards, can openers (manual and electric), spiral notebooks, and rulers also discriminate against the left-handed. Even the writing on pencils is upside down and backward for southpaws. Have you ever tried to wind a watch when the stem is pointing toward your elbow? Or have you ever tried to cut paper when all the scissors are good for is crinkling the paper? Pens with erasable ink can be just as frustrating—more ink winds on your hand than on your paper.

Products made expressly for left-handed people are hard to find; if they can be found at all, they are usually expensive. I sometimes wonder whether left-handed golf clubs for women aren't an endangered species. The clubs available are either the cheapest sets or the most expensive. Extra clubs for left-handed women, such as pitching wedges, sand wedges, and irons, are also hard to find.

One thing I would like to do is eat a meal without constantly bumping elbows with the person next to me. Another thing I would like to do is put a left-handed ladle in a punch bowl and watch the right-handers pour punch all over their arms—as I have done many times. But, I take solace from one fact: Since the right side of the brain controls the left side of the body, I must be in my right mind.

This writer has breathed life onto a piece of paper and has taken the time to be entertaining as well as say something important about herself. She sounds angry but in a positive way. Something about her anger delights the reader. It reminds me of television's Andy Rooney and his approach to ordinary, everyday experience.

In our next example, our author has presented himself in a positive upbeat fashion by proclaiming his joy at what most consider to be a highly arduous task:

I love to write. Being far from the most outgoing person in the world, writing gives me the opportunity to express my views and concerns as well as relax and, periodically, vent out my frustrations with paper and pen. Writing has limitless opportunities and experiments available where an author can use his powers of creation and imagination to their fullest. Writing is a field broad enough to satisfy my experimental, creative needs. Writing gives me pleasure and I would eventually like to write a book for publication. The challenges and obstacles writing entails make it intellectually stimulating as well as personally gratifying.

Just image how uplifting it would be to read the above essay deep into the process of reading applications where clearly the task of writing is something so painful even the reader senses the agony that the writers are feeling. What better way to stand out in a crowd of anguished people than to suddenly and surprisingly express one's joy at the task.

Personal experiences can be both interesting for the reader and a way to project a great deal of oneself onto a page:

One of the greatest changes in my life occurred during my high school years. My family moved from the city of Boston to the country. My parents wanted a change, one that would enable them to own and operate a country store (The Store). Talk about culture shock. I was stunned by the location into which we had moved. We had decided to rent a house on a farm. There was only one word to describe this place and that was RURAL. It took me a while to get over the fact that there were no shopping malls or cinemas around the corner, but instead I had to drive twenty to thirty miles to get to one. I was not able to use the telephone as I had wished because anywhere I had wanted to call was a long distance phone call. I had thought that the next four years were to be the most boring years of my life, but I was wrong.

During those four years of living in the country I developed many skills. The Store was a family business in which the children were expected to help out anyway they could. I was a cashier, a stockgirl, and even a gas pumper. Yes, that is right. I actually pumped gas for our customers in freezing weather. I worked long and hard hours at the store. However, it was for a good cause, my family. Working with the public in the store for four years made me realize I would never want to own and operate a country store myself. Not that I hated work, but it was a long and tiresome job that took up all of my free time. When we sold The Store this summer, I looked back on the past and realized it had not been a waste of time but a lifetime of experience crammed into four years of hard work.

This summer I did not have to work at The Store, therefore, I did part-time work on the farm where we live. Half of my summer was spent working in the fields. While working in the fields, I learned to bale hay, harvest the potato crop, and drive a tractor. I had been the only female the owners had ever hired to do work on this farm. Of all the summers I have lived here, I enjoyed this summer most. Since I have been living on this farm for four years, the doctors who own this place have come to know me very well. Last fall a calf was born whose mother had died while giving birth, and the doctors had a wonderful idea to name the calf after me. Personally, I could not see any resemblance whatsoever, but at least I know that when I move back to the city, there will still be a Jennifer on the farm.

This writer has admitted she had some adjustments to make moving to a farm and that she has overcome the challenges of hard physical labor. The personal touch at the end says this is a person of sensitivity and good humor.

———————

Here is another example of trauma caused by moving, a fairly common occurrence in today's mobile society:

It was painful and scary to leave my friends, school and all the securities of a home behind. Entering a new school, in a strange city, and seeing an endless sea of unfamiliar faces was enough to give me butterflies in my stomach every time I thought about it. I was lonely and unsure of myself so I tended to lean on my family more often for moral support and companionship than I previously had. Ironically, as a result, a closeness grew between my parents, brother, sister and I that will last as long as we live.

All the relatives we left behind were missed terribly so we made long excursions by car back to Washington every summer to visit. Traveling all over the country stopping at some of the most beautiful and historical sights in America was an exciting and unforgettable experience. The spectacular Grand Canyon, the wonders of Yellowstone National Park, and the magnificent redwood forests of California along with the historic Alamo and Washington DC are only a few of the marvelous spectacles I witnessed. I don't visit my relatives very often but I enjoy their company perhaps more than I would have if I saw them more frequently. I will always love to travel and also take pleasure in the visits with my relatives.

What stands out in my mind is that the writer has recognized the sunshine on a cloudy day. She looked at what seemed to be a negative event and realized the value of moving and the benefits of family closeness and travel opportunities it has provided. She continues with the following passage which reflects upon the impact of her trauma and how it has affected her personally:

> More important are the effects the changes have made in me as an individual. I am able to adjust easily to new environments because I have more self-confidence and I am more independent. Having left all my friends behind twice just to begin building a whole new set, I have become more outgoing and cordial. Knowing that I can and have started over from scratch to form solid, lasting friendships has given me a great deal of confidence in myself. Because I have gone through periods without recognizing a soul around me, I have been forced to spend a lot of time alone, learning to utilize this time to my advantage and not depend on constant companionship. I probably would not have encountered many solitary occasions until much later in my life had I not been forced to because of the situation I faced. Although I often find myself alone and have become very independent, I truly enjoy the company of other people and given an option would choose the latter more often than not.

———————

Have you ever heard of turning a bad thing into a good one? Here's what one young man said about his unsuccessful first attempt of the college admission process and the positive results it brought about:

> Last April I received the shock of my life. I was "shot down" by all the "elite" schools I applied to. I couldn't believe it. The next day I broke my shin playing soccer. It was a beauti-

ful weekend. I was never so depressed in my life. I started thinking to myself, as I lay in bed with a cast up to my thigh, 'I didn't deserve to go there anyway. I wish they would've given me the chance, though, I know I can succeed there! Well, hello Hometown State.'

Mom and Dad always told me I possessed good qualities and intelligence. Dad, especially, told me there was no way I'd get turned down. God, what an optimist. He said the admissions people would see what kind of person I was and what an addition I'd be to the school. The rejection was a slap in the face. But, today I am grateful. 'Thanks, I needed that.'

If nothing else, that weekend woke me up. I did a lot of thinking about my future and what road I was destined to travel. The way my luck was going, I felt sure the road would lead straight to the heart of Beirut. My dad had mentioned prep school to me a few months before, 'Just in case the impossible happened,' of course. Time and time again I told him, 'No way, Dad. I don't belong there.' I thought prep school was for rich kids and intellectuals. Boy, was I wrong. I attended one and I'm far from being either. Anyway, I decided to take up my father and his idea of attending Edgewood for one year. I had a long talk with my brother, who has always respected education and the opportunities available to one willing to put forth the effort and time. He told me education was not something to be rushed. 'Hell, Doug,' he said, 'You're only 18. What's your hurry?' I knew where he was coming from. What's a year to someone my age in the pursuit of the highest education he can get. Wait a minute. Did I say that? I could feel enthusiasm for education growing right there and then.

As a result of good essay writing and the benefits of a postgraduate year in a preparatory school, the above author was highly successful in gaining admission to several prestigious colleges.

This author impressed his college selection committee as a "no nonsense" individual. Although the writing borders on terse, his points are strongly and effectively presented.

> I think of myself as a very responsible person. My mother works three jobs and I'm never sure when she'll be home. I have a busy schedule myself, and sometimes our only contact is through notes left on the refrigerator. Sometimes I have to cook my own meals and I am expected to do my own laundry. When my mother is home, she is usually exhausted and doesn't want any aggravation. She doesn't want to remind me to clean up my room or take out the garbage, and most of the time she doesn't have to. All these things have helped me learn to be a self-starter.
>
> My parents have never been intrusive in my decision making. Although I am expected to do well in school, I am responsible for my own study habits. I choose which classes I take and I start school before my mother gets up in the morning. Being a self-starter has also affected my involvement with running. My mother has always been supportive and highly interested in my athletic endeavors; but she is not very knowledgeable about my sport. I don't mind explaining the rudiments of track to her though, because I know that she is proud of me for accomplishing so much on my own.

This essay clearly reflects a self-reliant young man who has established his independence. He takes pride in knowing he can react successfully to new situations. College admission deans can be certain he will make the transition to college and that his studies will in no way be affected by all the other adjustments he will have to make as a college freshman.

Here's an example of how painful memories can be presented in a positive way by emphasizing the lessons one has learned by going through a difficult time in one's life:

In order to learn who I am, one must know the manner in which I dealt with growing up. My childhood was not easy, and that was basically caused by my being overweight. I was already heavy for my age when I was approximately six years old. A lot of kids in school and my two older brothers teased me about it. The teasing continued until I was about eleven. These are just true facts. What was happening inside my head was important.

My peers were telling me I would never have any friends or be successful at anything. My two brothers and kids I thought were my friends told me the same thing so I could not help but believe it. I hated myself, and the pain of this was so great that I needed some form of release. Here, my sense of humor became helpful. I already had a knack for spontaneous jokes, and so my feelings came out through jokes about myself.

Another way I dealt with my feelings was through religion. I talked to God quite a lot, and just through hearing myself talk about my feelings, I defined a better understanding of them.

Now that that part of my life is over, I am able to see the changes I have been through and the person I have become. I can honestly say that I would not have had my childhood any other way. I am a firm believer in God and I still talk to Him, though now about positive things. I am open to new ideas and I welcome change. I know my feelings. I am honest with myself and do not feel guilty for having certain feelings. Because of this empathy, I do not judge others. I may not agree with them, but I understand them. I have a mind of my own. After being teased so much, the opinions of my peers are less important to me. I will never drink, smoke or take drugs, no matter what anyone else says.

I no longer make jokes about myself, but still have my sense of humor. After many hard years, I am finally able to say, 'I love me.'

━━━━━━━━

Here's another good example:

On one particular Sunday in church, two of my brothers started their usual squabbling. To separate them and thus end the disturbance, I simply changed seats with Stephen. I then heard the man in back of us comment to his wife what a responsibility he thought I had. I guess until then I had never thought about what my position as the oldest of ten children really meant. To the teachers who are bound to see more Jones' after me, I'm an example of what they may expect from our family. To my brothers and sisters I am a 'real-life senior' leaving behind a path of my accomplishments and mistakes to perhaps guide them through high school. To my parents I bring new problems not dealt with before only because there's no one before me. We've experimented and experienced together.

Living with so many varied personalities has taught me the valuable lesson of sharing: sharing material objects, sharing time for listening and speaking, sharing thoughts and events of the day, sharing rooms and dresser drawers, and sharing the household chores. My special situation in life has prepared me not only to make it through life at college away from home, but to enjoy the companionship of the many new acquaintances and perhaps make their stay a bit more relaxed and agreeable.

This writer will truly enjoy some of the liberating aspects of residential college life. Although she is proud of having developed so much responsibility for her family, she will also enjoy the opportunity of meeting new friends and making anxious people feel more relaxed about their first few days in college.

━━━━━━━━

Sometimes a time worn quotation can be used to launch an essay that really brings a writer to life on the printed page:

> Every morning, trying frustratedly to decide what to wear, I stand in front of my closet and a certain poster never fails to catch my attention. It reads, thanks to William Shakespeare, 'We know what we are but not what we may be.' In applying these words to myself, I find them to be almost too true, in that in spite of knowing what I am, I cannot even imagine what I may become in the future. I am a young adult attempting to establish my individual identity. In the process of doing so, I have and have had the opportunity to explore many unique directions.
>
> This past fall, for example, I had the chance to be a part of a political campaign. When Andrew Roberts ran for Delegate of the Montana Assembly, I was fortunate enough to find myself experiencing first hand the commitment that makes victory a reality. Before Election Day, we student volunteers found ourselves busy traveling to numerous shopping centers distributing palm cards and helium balloons. We were accompanied by Mr. Roberts, a lively politician, who practiced shaking hands and making impromptu speeches on passing audiences. On November 3rd, school was scheduled to open one hour late, and while many students slept that extra hour, we avid politicians were standing in the streets with more balloons, as well as picket signs, working that last minute before voters made their decisions final.

This is someone who gets so excited about the American political process he is willing to get up early in the morning and hand out balloons. What a lively person to bring to a college campus!

These next two essays are both in response to the request "please describe a single event or person who has had a significant impact on your life to date."

Note how both authors have chosen a very personal experience, not one that could have happened to anyone but themselves, nor one that will ever make the history books.

Last winter, I felt as if I wasn't participating enough in our school's extracurricular activities, so I started searching for a club or sport that would appeal to me. During a lunch break I asked a friend for suggestions; he told me he was involved in the school's track program as a pole vaulter during the spring, and the team was still one pole vaulter short. My search was over! All my life I've been drawn toward sports that are individualistic yet rigorously challenging, such as skiing, hiking and snorkeling. Thus, the following spring, I faithfully attended all of the track meetings and ardently ran the month long warm up program.

Finally, three and a half weeks later and eleven pounds lighter, the day I had anxiously been awaiting arrived. It was the day we pulled out the enormous mats and I was first instructed in the art of pole-vaulting. My dreams were shattered almost instantly as I realized the prodigious amounts of coordination, self-confidence and irrationality involved. My determination held, however, and little by little I began to improve. I was constantly admonished by my pole-vaulting colleagues that thinking was detrimental to one's performance in this particular sport and easily, I found they were correct.

I didn't actually make it over a bar, however, until several weeks later, during a critical track meet. Approximately nine schools participated in this meet and three vaulters were needed for a school to compete in the pole vault event. At this time I was the third vaulter, thus our coach signed our school up as a participant. The opening height a vaulter needed to clear for his jump to count was eight and a half feet. This, unfortunately, was at least three feet more than I'd ever vaulted, since I'd only recently mastered the "grip," the "plant," and the basics of "pop-up," all of which constitute only the bare essentials of pole vaulting.

As this was a relay, the heights cleared by each vaulter on

a team were to be added together, producing a final score for the team. The two other vaulters went first, both clearing awe-inspiring heights. When my turn arrived, I was mercilessly informed that if I cleared opening height, the eight and a half feet would give us second place, whereas if I failed, we would not place in the meet, and thus would not be eligible for the Regional competitions. One teammate pulled me aside and promised his eternal friendship if I was successful. With that, I took my place on the cement runway, said a quick prayer, and began sprinting like a mad-man. The next thing I knew, my feet were leaving the ground as I began my ascent. I felt myself soaring higher than I'd ever remembered, and as I looked down from my zenith, I saw the bar resting peacefully upon its delicate, but intimidating supports. I quickly released the pole and came tumbling down to the mats with a terrific smile on my face. The bar was still in place and my coach and teammates were cheering wildly. I had cleared the height, thus earning us an award.

I feel this experience was not only a team achievement, but also a personal one that has made a significant impact upon my life by giving me great confidence in myself. By proving I have the ability to realize if not conquer goals that may at first seem overwhelming, I have gained much courage and I have intensified my ambitions to succeed in all I do.

We all cheered with his teammates as this author cleared the pole vault bar. Anyone with this kind of determination and self-confidence will easily meet the new challenges presented by college life.

This next essay is a fine example of how powerful language can be in describing emotional build-up. Once again, note how the reader is grabbed by the author's first words.

"Awe shut up!" I screamed while slamming the car door. As the tires screeched and the car sped away, I mumbled to myself, "Sisters are the biggest pains." All morning we had been fighting over sweaters, to whom they belonged, how the bathroom should be kept, our hour of departure in order to arrive at school on time, and other important issues that two sisters so close in age usually fight about. In retaliation to my arguments that the red sweater was mine, the bathroom was a mess, and we did not have to leave for another five minutes; she had honked and honked rushing me at the last second just so she could make it on time. The car ride to school was even better as we both fumed, our anger toward each other building up rapidly. The dam holding the rising sea of heated emotions finally broke when I changed the radio stations and her hatred came flooding out, practically drowning me and my back pack, stopped only with the closing of the car door.

That incident occurred frequently in the past two years and seemed of great importance, but now is so trivial. How could I have wasted such precious time fighting? She has left for college, and with her went the laughter, the tears and that special security in knowing my sister would always be there. The old proverb, absence makes the heart grow fonder seemed unrealistic to me two years ago, but now it characterizes my thoughts and feelings for my sister. She has influenced my life greatly and has most importantly helped me grow as an individual.

My sister and I are foils to one another in all senses of the word. She has long blond hair, is very neat and tidy, loves to dress up, would rather watch sports than participate, and is very congenial to all. I am quite the opposite, with short, curly brown locks and an extraordinarily messy room. I always wear a uniform of jeans and a sweatshirt, play all sports, and am usually quite blunt, even when its the wrong thing to say. In addition to these differences, we attended rival high schools where tensions often ran high causing further ripples in our relationship. Our opposing characteristics enhanced our personalities and encouraged us to develop as individuals. . . .

Through her relationship with her sister, this author has learned much about dealing with people and benefiting from individual differences. One sentence, especially, "How could I have wasted such precious time fighting?" sums up what many people take a lifetime to realize. This kind of perception and maturity is welcome at our school.

━━━━━━━━

Keeping a log of one's daily schedule can often become a a very interesting story. Here's one from the College Counseling Seminar which is held at William and Mary each summer:

> 'Wake up!' screamed my Virginia roommate with the blonde punk haircut as she pounced onto my college bed/couch/desk in one. It was 6:00 a.m. and time to run down to the 2nd floor hallway of Monroe to the showers in order to beat the morning rush.
>
> 'Ughhh!' Cold water. Many dorm mates had obviously been here before me! After getting dressed in clothes that had been worn more than once, (cotton shrinks and besides that you do not know how to work the laundry machine, my roommate had warned me), my friends and I made the obstacle course morning dash to Trinkle Hall for breakfast. We had to get there before 7:15 to beat the squad of infantile obnoxious soccer players going to camp at William & Mary.
>
> 'Yum, yum!' Cold powdered eggs and black concrete sausages. I think I will stick to soft chocolate ice cream. With five minutes until class started, I set off towards Morton Hall for the first seminar.
>
> 'Arghhh!' Rain, I forgot I do not have mom to drive me to school. Soaked and defeated I arrive just in time. I put

out my schedule to review the day's activities:

Thursday, June 28

8:15 AM Decision Making: Strategies

9:45 AM Nuts and Bolts: The College Application & Visiting a College

1:00 PM Nuts and Bolts: How to Have a Good Interview

3:00 PM Group/Individual Counseling

7:00 PM Last Night Social

Inconspicuously I slip into a chair. The lecture begins.

'Admissions officers look for a few pertinent points during the interview: motivation, intellectual promise, energy level, sense of humor, values, stability, interest in college, oral communication skills, integrity, independence, and preparation.'

It is 3:00 p.m. and I have an appointment with Steve, my counselor. I will discuss what was taught this morning and also what research I have done on the colleges I am interested in. Picking a school is no easy task; I have been making up charts, reading every Barron's book and Selective Guide in print, and talking to other students from various schools that I am interested in. This week-long college counseling seminar has helped me narrow my choices and has taught me the application procedure. The purpose of this seminar was to simulate the first week of Freshman year at college. In it, we were given a roommate, able to live in a dorm, eat cafeteria food, attend classes and seminars and spend our free time as we pleased. We had activities such as a student/faculty volleyball game in which even the Dean of Admission of William and Mary, Mr. Gary Ripple, participated.

I learned the good and the bad of college life and unsurprisingly...I CAN'T WAIT!

11

Do's and Don'ts

DO'S

1. Plan ahead—leave time to write and rewrite your essays—with time in between. This will allow for fresh reviews and possible revisions of the original work.

2. Tell the truth about who you are and who you are not.

3. Tie yourself to the college: Explain why you are interested in attending and what the institution can do for you. Be specific. Go beyond "XYZ College will best allow me to realize my academic potential."

4. Read the directions carefully, follow them to the letter.

5. Consider the unique features of the institution. For example, a liberal arts college will be impressed with the variety of academic and personal interests you might have while an art school would be most interested in your creative abilities.

6. Be positive, upbeat and avoid the negatives. For example, do not write "I am applying to your school because I won't be required to take physical education and a foreign language."

7. Emphasize what you have learned. Remember to provide more than a narration when recounting an experience.

8. Write about something you know, something only you could write.

9. Make copies of everything, just in case.

10. Write something for the optional essays; the ones that ask if you'd like N. Choir State to know anything else about you.

DON'TS

1. Force it, be too funny, too sad, too cute, too silly "I enjoy playing the piano and guitar but not simultaneously").

2. Be redundant—essays should not be a rehash of information already provided on other parts of the application or on your high school transcript.

3. Let modesty cover up your greatest assets and achievements.

4. Worry about trick questions. Your readers are genuinely interested in your answers to the questions.

5. Be afraid to confess your anxieties or indecisiveness. Admission officers are people who enjoy helping people and can be quite moved by the knowledge that you need them.

6. Use any of these ideas (or similar ones):

"Webster's Seventh New Collegiate Dictionary defines courage as 'mental or moral strength to venture, persevere, and withstand danger...''

"The following list gives a pretty good idea of the person I really am:"

"I think it is totally unfair of you to ask me to write about myself because it is so hard to that it hurts."

"I think you have no right to ask all these questions because you don't care about the answer—you just look at SAT scores!"

PART VI

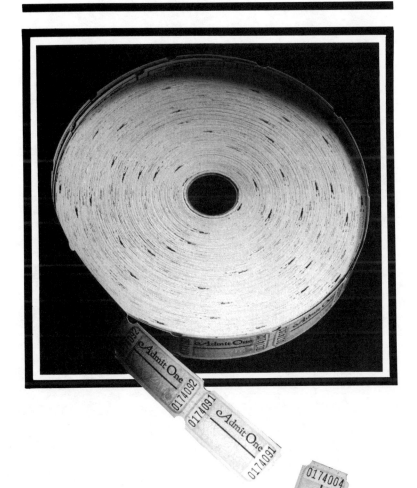

Questions Interviewers Might Ask You

I. WHAT ARE YOUR GOALS?

—What will be the "good life" for you twenty years from now?

—How do you define success? Are you satisfied with your accomplishments to date?

—Why do you work hard (not so hard)?

—Have you set any academic goals for yourself so far? Have you met them? If not, why not?

—What are your college and career goals?

II. HOW WELL DO YOU KNOW YOURSELF—YOUR STRENGTHS/WEAKNESSES?

—If I visited your school for a few days, what would I find is your role in the school community? What would your teachers say were your greatest strengths as a person, as a student; likewise, what about your shortcomings or weaknesses?

—What kind of self-development do you wish to see in yourself in the next four years?

—In a sentence or two, what points about yourself would you like to leave with me so that I can present your strongest side to our committee on admissions?

—What kind of person would you like to become? Of your particular gifts and strengths, which would you most like to develop? What would you most like to change about yourself?

—How do you learn best? Do you do best in a competitive atmosphere? Do you work best independently or with others? Are you self-motivated or do you need close personal attention from your teachers?

—What extracurricular activities at school have been most important to you? Have you shown any special commitment to or competence in them? What about activities outside school? What's the relative importance to you of academics vs. extracurricular activities?

—How would others describe your role in either your school or your home community? Do you feel you have made any significant contribution in either area?

—Perhaps the toughest question of all: Would your best friend, your parents, or your school counselor agree with the picture of yourself as you have just described it (if your answer is no, maybe you'd better do some more thinking!)?

—Do you believe that you are adequately prepared for a college curriculum?

—How confident are you about your writing skills? How often do you write a paper?

—At what are you best?

—What one trait is your most important?

—Has there been an important experience in your life that has contributed the most to your maturing process or understanding yourself?

—What have you learned about yourself and/or other people from experience X (for example, a leadership position, or moving several times while growing up)?

III. WHAT ARE YOUR VALUES? HOW HAVE THEY BEEN FORMED OR CHANGED?

—Do you have contemporary heroes? Historical heroes?

—What events would you deem crucial in your life thus far?

—Describe some things that have really made you indignant over in the past year.

—If I could hand you my telephone and let you talk to any one person living, to whom would you like to talk? Why?

—If I said you had $10,000 to spend in a year between high school and college, how would you spend the money and time?

—If you were chosen as the new principal in your high school, what would be your first move?

—What events or experiences in your life so far have had the greatest influence on your growth and thinking—on making you the person you are today?

—What have you enjoyed most about your high-school experience? If you could live these last few years over again, what would you do differently?

—Which relationships are most important to you? Why? Describe your best friends. Are they mostly similar to or different from you?

—How has your environment—school, family, the town you live in—influenced your way of thinking? Have they mostly served to expand or to circumscribe your life and activities?

—What bothers you the most about the world around you? If you had the opportunity and the responsibility to change the world, where would you start?

—What have you gained from your (athletic, school, club, etc.) activities?

IV. INDIVIDUALITY

—What pressures do you feel operating on you in society to conform? Describe ways in which you and your friends "go your own way."

—What do you feel sets you apart as an individual in your school?

—Have you ever thought of not going to college? What would you do?

V. INTELLECTUAL INTERESTS AND POTENTIAL

—Where and when do you find yourself most stimulated intellectually?

—What books or articles have made a lasting impression on your way of thinking? Have you read deeply into any one author or field?

—What are your academic interests and preferences? Which subjects and courses have you enjoyed the most? Which have been the most difficult for you?

—Briefly describe your course of study.

—Which are your favorite subjects? Why?

—How much time do you spend in study/preparation/homework each night?

—What subjects are hardest for you? Easiest?

—What subject is your favorite? Your least favorite? Why?

—Tell me about your musical interests.

—Do you write outside of school? What type of things?

—Describe a project or assignment that you particularly enjoyed and how you went about completing it.

—If you had to convince someone who hates (insert student's favorite subject) that it can be worthwhile and interesting to study, what would you say?

VI. INTEREST IN SCHOOL; ABILITY TO CONTRIBUTE TO SCHOOL

—What is the most significant contribution you've made to your school?

—What do you feel that you have to offer (Name of College)?

—What characteristics of a college do you consider to be most important?

—How much prior research and investigation have you done about (Name of College)?

—Why did you choose the particular activities you did?

—How often do you write for the school newspaper and how often does it come out?

—What activities might you pursue further if you came to (Name of College)?

—Why a liberal arts college? Why (Name of College)?

—What factors will you weigh most heavily in deciding to which colleges to apply?

—What kind of environment do you want in college?

—What are you looking for in a university?

VII. OTHERS

—What have you read, seen, or heard about (Name of College) that you don't like? What rumors can I confirm or deny?

—Is there anything you'd like to toss into the interview as a parting comment?

—After a long, hard day, what do you most enjoy doing? What do you do for fun? For relaxation?-

—What are the major problems at your high school these days?

—How would you rate the quality of instruction at your school?

—How would you evaluate the counselling services of your school?

—How do you spend your summers and vacation periods?

—How do you feel about your most recent grades?

—How demanding is your secondary school?

—How do you feel about your current teachers? Which one is most exciting? Why?

—Have you won any academic awards or earned any particular academic recognition?

—Is there anything more you'd like to tell me about your academic record?

—Have you earned any varsity letters?

—What have been the satisfactions and frustrations with some of your leadership roles?

—Is there anything that we've not talked about that you would like to discuss? Is there anything that we have discussed that you'd like to tell me more about?

—Can you subtract 1/5 from 1/3 mentally?

—What have you read for fun recently?

—What would you do if you didn't get into any of the schools to which you'd made application?

—When you think of the best educated people you know as friends, or friends of your family, what are the characteristics which are most impressive? How do you connect those qualities with the kind of education they have pursued?

Questions to Ask the College

I. GENERAL INFORMATION:

—How many students will be in your freshman class this year?

—What is the average class size in the freshman year? Overall?

—What are the smallest class sizes? The largest?

—Are there televised courses?

—Do graduate students teach undergraduates?

—Do faculty maintain office hours?

—Are students involved in the evaluation of instructors?

—What percent of the faculty is tenured?

—Do professors have any policy on class attendance?

—How is registration handled?

—Are certain courses hard to get into? What percent?

—How much time is allotted between classes?

—What is the farthest distance between academic buildings?

—Is there an honor code? Does it work?

—How are students advised about which courses to take?

—How far are you from the nearest airport? Train station? Bus?

—Do you provide transportation locally? To airports? Trains?

II. DORM LIFE

—What percentage of your students are housed on campus?

—What percent live off-campus? Commute from home?

—How many students are assigned to a room?

—Are the bathrooms public or private?

—Are there coed dorms? By floor? Wing? How?

—What services are provided in dorms? (Kitchens, laundry, service, linen, air conditioning, etc.)

—How are roommates chosen? Can I room with a friend?

—What if my roommate and I do not get along?

—Are freshmen required to be on campus? In all freshman dorms?

—How does your resident advisor system function?

—Are there telephones in each room? Optional?

III. FOOD SERVICE

—Do you have your own food service or an outside caterer?

—Must I purchase a meal ticket? How many meals per week?

—Is there a salad bar? Choice of entrees?

—Are special diets available?

—What about between meals and evening snacks?—What is the average weight gain in the freshman year?

IV. FINANCIAL AID

—Will applying for financial aid have any impact on admissions decisions? What about students placed on the waiting list?

—What costs does the college budget cover? Are transportation and personal expenses includes?

—How is financial aid awarded to students?

—Is financial aid based on need? Based on merit?

—Are all students' needs met completely? If not, whose need is met? How much of their need is met?

—What happens after freshman year?

—Do special groups (athletes, musician, legacies, minority students) receive special treatment?

—What are the institution's policies regarding divorces/separated families?

—How many students receive financial aid? Scholarship aid?

—What are the financial aid application procedures and deadlines?

What forms must be submitted? What are the procedures for Early Decision applicants?

—When do students learn about their financial aid package?

—How and why might extensions be provided for the May 1 reply date?

—What employment opportunities are available for students not receiving financial aid?

—Does the institution have an installment payment plan? What about other financing options?

V. OTHER

—If our roles were reversed, what would you like to know about me so that you could make an intelligent and fair decision on my application for admission or, better still, on my competence as your interviewer?

—What differentiates your school from all of the other small liberal arts institutions?

—What is the school's endowment per student?

—What kinds of personal qualities do students here tend to have? How can I tell if I would fit in?

—In what ways do your students attribute their growth to their (Name of College) education?

—What is the philosophy, mission, purpose of the University?

—If you could change something about the University, what would you change?

Name of College:	Type (e.g., 4-year liberal arts, 2-year community college, etc.):	Test(s) required:	Score report(s) due:	Admission Application deadline:	Financial Aid Application deadline:	Total annual expenses:	Amount of financial aid available:	Total undergraduate enrollment: Women: Men:	Freshman class— Number that applied: Number that were accepted: Number that enrolled:

Campus Visit Checklist

- [ ] **Call Ahead (Don't Write) and Ask About**
    - [ ] Appointment for interview
    - [ ] Tour times
    - [ ] Distance/directions
    - [ ] Special accommodations
        - [ ] Food   [ ] Housing   [ ] Classes
    - [ ] What to bring
    - [ ] Information that can be mailed to you in advance

- [ ] **Prepare and Agenda**
    - [ ] What do I need to know about the college?
        - [ ] List of questions
    - [ ] What do I want the college to learn about me?
        - [ ] Resume   [ ] Transcript   [ ] Portfolio

- [ ] **The Visit Should Include:**
    - [ ] Plenty of time
    - [ ] Interview/tour
    - [ ] Sit in on a class
    - [ ] Try the food
    - [ ] Meet a professor
    - [ ] Pick up information and application
    - [ ] Free time to stroll and browse

- [ ] **After the Visit**
    - [ ] Make notes to refresh your memory later on
    - [ ] Jot down lingering questions
    - [ ] Thank you note

College Trivia

Answers

1. Tarleton State University, Stephenville, Texas.
2. Arkansas College, Batesville, Arkansas.
3. The College of William and Mary, Williamsburg, Virginia.
4. The Marriott Library at the University of Utah, July, 1986.
5. The University of Chicago, Chicago, Illinois.
6. Northwestern University, Evanston, Illinois.
7. 1901.
8. Washington and Lee University (then just Washington College), Lexington, Virginia.
9. Westminster College, Fulton, Missouri. On March 5, 1946 Churchill spoke these now famous words "From Stettin in the Balic to Trieste in the Atlantic, an iron curtain has descended across the continent."
10. Knox College, Galesburg, Illinois.
11. Bowdoin College, Maine and Ohio University, Ohio. The year was 1828.
12. In 1755, the University of Pennyslvania (Philadelphia, Pennsylvania) became the first school in America to be founded as a university.
13. The University of Chicago, Chicago, Illinois.
14. The University of Kansas, Lawrence, Kansas.
15. Amherst College, Amherst, Massachusetts and Williams College, Williamstown, Massachusetts. The game was played in 1859. Amherst was ahead 73 to 32 when the game was called due to darkness.
16. The University of Southern California, Los Angeles, California.
17. Texas Christian University, Texas.
18. Lafayette College, Pennsylvania.
19. Ward Landrigan graduated from Drew University in Madison, New Jersey in 1963.

20. Drew University, Madison, New Jersey.
21. Carleton College, Northfield, Minnesota.
23. The Wilson Commons at The University of Rochester, New York. Designed by I.M. Pei, the Wilson Commons atrium contains 18,000 square feet of glass, trees from Florida, and yes, a family of lizards.
24. Williams College, Williamstown, Massachusetts.
25. South Dakota School of Mines, Rapid City, South Dakota.
26. Cleary College, Ypsilanti, Michigan. It was founded in 1883 with an initial enrollment of two students.
27. Oberlin College, Oberlin, Ohio.
28. Colby College, Waterville, Maine (in 1871).
29. Brandeis, Waltham, Massachusetts.
30. These men both graduated from Kenyon College in Gambier, Ohio.
31. Hampden-Sydney College in Hampden Sidney, Virginia.
32. Kappa Alpha Theta was founded at Depauw University in Greencastle, Indiana.
33. These are all clubs at Sweet Briar College in Sweet Briar, Virginia.
34. Mary Washington College in Fredericksburg, Virginia.
35. Saint Vincent College, Latrobe, Pennsylvania.

Money Saving Guides and Services from Octameron

TITLE, PRICE & DESCRIPTION

Don't Miss Out: The Ambitious Student's Guide To Financial Aid. $4.50
Hailed in *Money, Forbes,* & the *NY Times* as the nation's top consumer guide to student aid. Updated yearly, it covers scholarships, grants, loans and personal finance techniques. It's also the first to spot new trends and new opportunities. Guaranteed to save the sophisticated reader hundreds, if not thousands, of dollars in college costs.

The As & Bs of Academic Scholarships. $4.50
Money for being bright! Over 100,000 merit awards offered by 1200 colleges described in full detail. Best of all, most of the scholarships are not based on financial need. Also included, the major merit awards sponsored by Uncle Sam, the states, and private groups.

College Grants From Uncle Sam: Am I Eligible And For How Much? $2.25
Almost 70% of all families are eligible for college help under federal grants. You'll get program descriptions, the ins and outs of applications, plus easy worksheets that will show you how much help you can expect.

College Loans From Uncle Sam: The Borrower's Guide That Explains It All. $2.25
Do you know how to increase your eligibility for a low-interest loan? Where to find little-known information about loan deferments and loan forgiveness? Loans for students, parents, and health professionals—they are all described in this compact guide.

Earn & Learn: Cooperative Education Opportunities With the Federal Government. $2.75
Here's a painless way to pay for college! Alternate formal studies with work for Uncle Sam. Jobs exist in nearly every career field. At $7.00+/hour. At the associate, baccalaureate, and graduate levels. And when you finish, a government job is waiting for you!

Financial Aid Officers: What They Do—To You And For You. $2.75
When the college offers you an aid award, should you accept it? Can you request that the award's composition be changed—more grants, less loans—or that the award be increased? How much negotiating leeway do you have? Knowledgeable dealings with financial aid officers can improve your package. FAO gives you a candid discussion of this strategy.

Behind The Scenes: An Inside Look At The Selective College Admission Process. $2.75
Ed Wall, former Dean of Admission at **Amherst College,** answers questions on selective admissions, dispenses sage advice, and provides detailed profiles of successful applicants. An invaluable view from the inside and "must reading" for all those who seek entrance to the nation's top schools.

Top Dollars For Technical Scholars: A Guide To Engineering, Math, Computer Science, and Science Scholarships. $4.25
You'll find detailed scholarship listings, advice on how to compete successfully for awards, and information about the future of technical studies. Also explains how technical scholarships can lead to future employment.

College Check Mate: Innovative Tuition Plans That Make You A Winner. $4.50
Don't pay full price for college! In response to rapidly rising tuition rates, many schools have developed assistance plans to help ease the payment burden for families at all income levels. Check Mate describes dozens of these plans as they exist at hundreds of our nation's schools.

Update Service. $3.00
Suppose Congress or the Administration changes all the ground rules for student aid in mid-stream? How will you know about it? Easy. Register with our update service. Between now and September 1988 we'll let you know of any approved major changes—as often as they occur.

We Can Help You.   Free.
Do you need personalized help with college selection, admission, or financial aid? Could you use the advice of experts whose views are sought by the *NY Times* and the *Money Magazine*? We offer many different services. They are described in the free brochure **WE CAN HELP YOU.**

Books may be ordered from:

OCTAMERON ASSOCIATES, P.O. BOX 3437, ALEXANDRIA, VA 22302
Please include 75¢ per publication to a maximum of $3.75 for postage and handling.